The Deaf Murders

(those who killed and those killed)

Peter W. Jackson

First published in Great Britain 2015

Copyright © Peter Jackson 2015

Published by
Deafprint Winsford
Winsford
Cheshire
CW7 3UD
England

British Library Cataloguing Data

ISBN 978-0-9562288-4-0

Printed in England by Orbital Digital Print Services, Sittingbourne, Kent ME10 2NH

To

Carol & Marilyn

(Lost then found after 57 years!)

Other Crime Books by Peter Jackson

Deaf Crime Casebook
Deaf to Evidence
Deaf Murder Casebook
Deaf Target
Death Around the Green
Deaf Killers
Deaf Injustices
Deaf Executions
The Deaf to Deaf Killings
Deaf Renegades, Outlaws, Cop Killers & other murders

History Books

Britain's Deaf Heritage
A Pictorial History of Deaf Britain
A History of the Deaf Community in Northwich and Winsford 1880 –
2002
(with Maureen Jackson)
Deaf Lives (Ed. with Raymond Lee)
Manchester Memoirs (Ed.)
Preston Pride (with Maureen Jackson)
The Gawdy Manuscripts
Nightingale Lane
The Origins of the British Deaf Association (with Raymond Lee)
Alexander Popham's Notebook

Contents

BOOK TWO: Those who got killed...

Introduction & Acknowledgements

I didn't think I would write any more crime books but many other people kept feeding me stories or titbits of murders and crimes that happened to Deaf people or which were committed by Deaf people.

Also, in the last three years, there were two very high profile murder cases in the Deaf Community in Britain and friends kept passing to me newspaper articles or other information about these cases. In the end, however, I could not even write about them because the Deaf people who went on trial for these deaths or killings were found not guilty of the deaths, one of which was deemed an unfortunate accident.

My thanks in this particular book go to Corrie Tijsseling of the Netherlands for her contribution and translation from Dutch to English of the 1988 case from the Netherlands.

Similarly, a lady who prefers to remain anonymous was very helpful in translating the Belgian case of 1991, and Ravi Ashwan contributed to the Indian case of 2013.

I am also grateful to Steve Hooker of Christchurch, New Zealand for his assistance in providing information relating to Hedley Nye and Emma Agnew.

It has been a great pleasure researching and writing all about Deaf crime and Deaf murders but reluctantly, the time has come to stop with the issue of this book, as I feel I have exhausted many of the older cases that could be written about.

I will continue to write crime stories in main stream magazines such as *True Crime, True Detective, Master Detective* and *Murder Most Foul* but these articles will most likely be mainstream crime stories, such as the one I researched and wrote about whilst in Ohio in 2012. *The Bodies in the Tree* was an unusual case where a murderer who was a tree surgeon dumped the bodies of three victims and their dog down a hollowed out tree trunk from a height of 40 feet. These bodies would never have been found if the murderer had not been found holding one of the victims' daughter hostage and confessed where he had dumped her mother, her friend and her brother.

I will look for more cases like that in order to carry on writing.

To all my faithful readers and connoisseurs of Deaf Murder, thank you for your support over the past 18 years since I first wrote *Deaf Crime Casebook.*

Peter W. Jackson
Winsford
May 2015

A Melancholy Homicide, *Kilmore, Co. Down, Ireland 1851*

Thomas Dunlop, described as a decent-looking man, had a liking for drink and was sometimes seen around his village of Kilmore where the family had a farm, frequently intoxicated. This was the case on Saturday 30 August 1851 when Thomas Dunlop entered the whiskey shop of Catherine Savage and signed for some whisky.

Already in the shop was Dunlop's brother, Francis, and a family friend, Samuel Stewart. Knowing that Thomas was frequently penniless, and perhaps not wanting to add to his drunkenness, Catherine Savage looked at Francis for advice. With a sigh, Francis told the shopkeeper to give him half a pint.

Shortly afterwards, Stewart and the two brothers left the shop and walked towards the brothers' house where they went in, leaving Stewart to continue to his own house. Inside the Dunlop house, there was another brother Alexander and a sister, Nancy, both of whom were also Deaf. There was also a Deaf cousin present, Jane Cleland and her friend Thomas Walker.

Immediately there was an argument between Thomas and Jane Cleland because of a derogatory sign she directed towards Thomas, accusing him of being drunk. This argument was soon smoothed over, and dinner was prepared, which Thomas Walker was invited to share with the family. Walker declined, but was pushed by Thomas Dunlop into the dining area and they all sat down to eat.

During the meal, another argument started, this time between the brothers about some money, and Francis kicked Thomas under the table, hitting him on the knee.

The two Thomases then got up and left the table, but Francis followed them intent on continuing the argument. Francis signed to his brother that he wanted him, but Walker got between them and told Francis to leave his brother alone. However, Francis persisted in signing to Thomas and they both went out of the kitchen together.

Shortly afterwards, Walker heard a scuffle in the hall and the noise of a pane of glass being broken. When Walker went to investigate, he saw that Thomas was on the floor and Francis was continually hitting him. After Walker managed to pull Francis off Thomas, he got Thomas out into the street but the enraged brother was still not finished with Thomas Dunlop, striking him a severe blow on the nose which caused blood to flow. Further punches were thrown at Thomas who tried to avoid them.

Walker then got between the brothers again and pushed Francis back into the house. Thomas Dunlop followed the two into the house still bleeding from the nose and he was seen to put his hand into the knife box, and taking a knife, Thomas suddenly rushed at Francis and thrust it into his abdomen.

As Francis cried out that he was stabbed, Thomas Walker and Alexander Dunlop jumped on Thomas and succeeded in getting the knife off him before he could inflict more damage on his brother.

When Thomas Dunlop ran out of the house, the doctor was sent for but Francis died of his wound at 10 o'clock the next morning, and Thomas Dunlop was soon arrested and charged with the murder of his brother.

The post mortem was carried out by Robert Forde, MD, who told the inquest held on 6 September 1851 that he had found two wounds on the surface of the body of the victim. One was on the left side of the abdomen, about an inch long, which penetrated the stomach. The other was a defensive wound on Francis Dunlop's right forearm. The cause of death was a sharp instrument entering the stomach causing an internal haemorrhage.

The court had some difficulty in obtaining statements not only from Thomas but also his Deaf relatives who had witnessed the fight between the brothers. There were so many Deaf people and others who could use sign language who could not be used to interpret the statements at the inquest. because they were either witnesses or stood accused.

The Coroner, Mr. B. Ward, Esq., then remanded Thomas Dunlop to be remanded in gaol until the next Assizes to be held at Downpatrick Crown court, which would be the following March.

When the trial commenced, some difficulty was experienced in getting the accused to plead. Dunlop persisted in signing to his brother Alexander across the court that it was all Francis' fault, and refused to admit that he had stabbed his brother.

After asking if Thomas Dunlop could read and write and being told that while he could, he might not understand the content, the Judge directed that a plea of 'not guilty' be entered on his behalf, and appointed a man named James McTeer, who knew a way of communicating with the defendant by signs, to interpret not only Thomas Dunlop's testimony but also those of the Deaf witnesses who would be called to provide evidence. This resolved the interpreting problems that had come about in the inquest.

How Thomas Dunlop might have looked in the dock

Mr. Crawford, representing Thomas Dunlop, argued in a very able manner that because of the injuries inflicted on Thomas by his brother, who had started the affray first, it was surely to the benefit of Thomas that he committed the act (of knifing his brother) to put a stop to the repeated assaults. The court had heard from the witness, Thomas Walker, that he had to interfere in the assault twice to pull Francis away from his brother. Therefore what Thomas had done was justifiable homicide.

The Judge agreed, but said there was still the fact Thomas had picked up the knife. Without that fact, Francis would still be alive.

Without leaving the jury box, the jury returned a verdict of guilty of manslaughter, and Thomas Dunlop was then sentenced to a prison term of 12 months.

The Trial of William Sturt, *Brighton, England 1863*

A widower and a painter by trade, William Sturt lived in the Kemptown area of Brighton with some of his six children by his late wife Charlotte who had died several years previously. Aged 49 and profoundly deaf but with fairly good speech, Sturt had started going out with a widow, Mary Ann Day who had nine children still living with her in rooms at 14 Rock Street, St. James Street, Brighton. A straw-bonnet maker by trade, Mary had fallen on hard times and had a liking for drink, often frequenting a drinking house run by a woman named Jutton. The drinking house was known to most people in Brighton as Jutton's.

Sturt himself had gone downhill since his wife died and had began to neglect his once-prosperous painting business, and also began frequenting Jutton's where he met Mary. They began going out together, spending most of their time in the various drinking houses around Brighton - mostly Jutton's.

By and large, the couple got on well although William Sturt would complain at times of Mary's association with several young men. Possibly he was not aware that she was getting money from them for sex in order to fund her drinking. They got on so well that by February 1863, there were plans for them to get married in the May of that year.

On Sunday 22 February, William Sturt called at Mary Day's lodgings, as was his custom to go out with her to Jutton's. She informed him she was not feeling well, and he gave her a drink of gin. They then left the house together about mid-day, and on the way to Jutton's, Mary Day said she was a bit hungry.

Sturt then produced a mince pie from his coat pocket, saying that he had bought it at eleven o'clock the previous night from a shop run by a woman named Elizabeth Wilding in George Street, and it had been in his pocket since then. Soon after eating it, Mary Day said she felt quite ill, with a sensation of burning in her throat and nausea.

Although they had a beer at Jutton's, Mary complained that she was still feeling quite ill, so they set off back to her lodgings. On the way, she was sick and upon arriving home she was put to bed by her two older daughters, Amelia and Sophia, who told Sturt to leave the house.

Mary Day spent the day wracked with pain, constantly vomiting and purging herself, and when Sturt called again between 7 and 8 pm, she told him that she had suffered greatly since eating that mince pie. Sturt gave her a brandy and water to drink but did not suggest that a doctor be called, neither did her daughters who shooed him out of the house again.

Mary Day died at 10:30 that night, still in agony, and at an inquest held the next day, the coroner stated that the death was so suspicious that he was forwarding samples of her stomach contents to a Professor Taylor for a proper analysis in order to ascertain the true cause of death. He also ordered that the rest of the mince used in the making of Elizabeth Wilding's pies should also be analysed.

George Street, Brighton in the 1900s.
William Sturt bought a mince pie from Elizabeth Wilding's shop in this street.

As a result of the analysis report received from Professor Taylor, William Sturt was brought up before the magistrates on Wednesday morning and formally indicted with allegedly causing the death of Mary Day by poisoning her. The report stated there was enough white arsenic in her body to cause the deaths of several people.

This poison, white arsenic, was commonly used for agricultural purposes in the district and it was suggested that it would not have been difficult for William Sturt to have obtained it.

Sturt was committed for trial at the next assizes in Lewes and refused bail and sent to gaol in the same town to await his trial, which was held on Thursday 26 March 1863.

William Sturt was asked how he pled, and he replied in a loud voice, "Not Guilty."

Much was made at the trial of the fact that Sturt had purchased a pie late at night and left it in his coat pocket all night before giving it to Mary Day the next day for her lunch. As the pie had been fully consumed, it had not been possible for it to be analysed. However, the rest of the mince used in Mrs. Wilding's pies had tested negative for arsenic, and it was alleged that if the pie was indeed the cause of the arsenic poisoning, William Sturt had ample time while in possession of it overnight to introduce arsenic into it.

The owner of the drinking house, Jutton, told the court that Sturt had told him he was thinking of not going through with the forthcoming marriage, complaining that Mary Day had lied to him about her age and the number of children that she had. Mary Ann Day was also more poverty-stricken than Sturt had realised, and the methods whereby she obtained her money were questionable. Sturt complained about her association with the young man who worked in the local railway station and other young men she had been seen with in the district behind his back, suggesting that she was providing sexual favours for money.

It was alleged that there was a very large quantity of white arsenic in Mary's body which could have only got there by eating the pie given to her by William Sturt.

However, a doctor suggested that as Mary Day suffered greatly from rheumatic pains, it was possible that she had been using arsenic for medical purposes. This belief that the use of arsenic to treat rheumatism was common in women at the time.

The judge told the jury that there was insufficient proof William Sturt had deliberately intended to murder Mary Day and a Not Guilty verdict was recorded in court.

William Sturt walked free from court. He continued to live the life of a pauper, and died in Brighton's Race Hill workhouse in 1883.

A Premature Verdict, *Vaucluse, France 1876*

Vaucluse is a department in the south-east of France. The area contains the famous Provence city of Avignon, and the area is characterised by small villages of closely built houses dating many hundreds of years and villages perched on hilltops.

There, in the small hamlet of Valzon lived a Deaf watchmaker named Plantévin and his Deaf wife. In their house, there lodged another Deaf man named Eustéze Recördan, who was - as villagers went - a man of means who plied a trade as a moneylender.

All three Deaf people had known each other for many years, having attended the same school for the deaf in Marseille. Their friendship had also lasted many years until the watchmaker Plantévin found himself in some business difficulty and approached Monsieur Recördan for financial assistance. The 500 francs that Plantévin received from M. Recördan was regarded by the watchmaker and his wife as a gift, but to M. Recördan it was a straightforward business loan that would have to be paid back within a specific period.

When no repayment was forthcoming from Plantévin, the moneylender employed his usual method of collecting the debt by sending a sheriff's officer to execute a warrant for the recovery of the debt.

Whilst Plantévin was taken aback when confronted by the sheriff's officer and settled the debt immediately, Madame Plantévin took umbrage at the effrontery of M. Recördan demanding settlement of his debt through a sheriff's officer, bringing shame on the Plantévins.

A Corsican by birth and steeped in the traditional ways regarding how disputes were settled in Corsica where resort to court action and ligation were regarded as unmanly, she swore revenge on M. Recördan for the humiliation suffered at his hands.

Firstly, M. Recördan was kicked out of his lodgings with the Plantévins, his belongings dumped in the street and told to find somewhere else to live. Shortly afterwards, the moneylender was found in an alleyway lying in a large pool of blood with his head smashed in. He had not been robbed because he still had on his person his purse with several hundreds of francs.

A typical alleyway in Vaucluse where the moneylender Eustéze Recördan was found dead lying in a pool of blood.

Naturally, Monsieur and Madame Plantévin became the prime suspects as their new feud with M. Recördan was common knowledge in the small town, and the fact that Madame Plantévin had sworn revenge on the moneylender for the humiliation that he had heaped upon her and her husband was also common knowledge.

There was also the fact that two hammers belonging to the watchmaker and a white linen apron that Madame Plantévin was known to be in the habit of wearing were missing.

The wheels of French justice however turn very slowly, and it was not until 25th April 1876 that the Deaf couple appeared before the assize court in Vaucluse accused of M. Recördan's murder.

Monsieur and Madame Plantévin were allowed to give evidence through the services of two interpreters, but on the third day of the trial, Madame Plantévin lodged an objection with the presiding judge, saying that the interpretation given of what they were saying was incorrect. After checking with a different interpreter and finding that the two interpreters had not translated the facts correctly in court, the judge moved to declare the trial void and to reconvene at the next assizes in August. Before he could do so, the Plantévins withdrew their complaint of misinterpretation to allow the trial to continue.

At that point, the foreman of the jury made it known to the judge that he and his fellow jurors had already made up their minds that the verdict was to be one of acquittal. The judge declared that the due process of law had been violated, and that the trial had to take place all over again, with a fresh jury.

The second trial was speedily concluded, and both the Plantévins were found guilty. It was held by the jury and confirmed by the judge that Madame Plantévin was the instigator of the crime, having publicly sworn revenge on M. Recördan in a typically Corsican manner. She was condemned to twenty years' penal servitude.

Monsieur Plantévin was declared to be a man who lacked sufficient will-power to resist an invitation to murder the moneylender and held to be less to blame. Nonetheless, for his part in the murder, he was sentenced to eight years penal servitude.

The Orphan treated as a slave, *Paris, France 1891*

Samuel Binns was an orphan. He was also Deaf and unable to speak at all and said to be of fairly low intelligence and not able to look after himself although he was now 21 years of age. His inability to look after himself may also have been compounded by the fact that, although English, he lived in France with a family that treated him with contempt.

When he was about 12 years old and living in Derbyshire in England, his parents were both killed in a house fire which left young Samuel Binns both homeless and orphaned. After a spell living in a workhouse, a Madame Gorse arrived from France and presented herself to the authorities as the sister of the late Mrs. Binns. Her information was accepted at face value by the local Poor Law guardians and she was allowed to adopt the boy and take him out of the country to Paris where she had a milliner's shop as well as a small farm on the outskirts.

Samuel Binns was put to work on the farm. He was not paid a wage, but was provided with sleeping quarters in a barn alongside the cows, pigs and hens. His food was simply the leftovers from the family dining table and Madame Gorse, who was a widow, proved to be a stern taskmaster making the young Samuel work really hard.

Occasionally, Binns was ordered to give a hand in moving Madame Gorse's stock from her shop to various customers, and transferring stock from the nearest train station, Gare de St. Lazare, to her shop. In time, Binns got to know the route between the station and the milliner's shop quite well and sometimes went on his own. These trips were just about the only "freedom" he had from the tyranny of Madame Gorse.

Madame Gorse had three children of her own from her deceased husband. The two older children, both girls aged 16 and 18, worked for their mother in her milliners business, mostly in the dressmaking rooms attached to the shop. The younger child, a boy aged 15, theoretically worked on the farm but was so lazy that he forced Samuel to do most of the work that had to be done, and tried to do as little as possible. When Binns complained about the son's idleness, he was beaten with a whip by Madame Gorse, a large woman of fearsome temper, much to the amusement of the other three children. In time, Samuel Binns grew to intensely dislike the other three children for the favours they were constantly being shown by their mother.

The only kindness that Binns received from anyone in the locality was from a family named Brusson. The 19-year-old daughter especially sometimes went out of her way to give Binns some treats and once intervened when the Gorse son's bullying of the Deaf boy got too much.

One day, it was made known to Binns that the Brusson family would be leaving France. They were going to a new life in Buenos Aires, Argentina.

The daughter drew pictures for Binns to show what they were going to do so that he understood they would be going away and that he would not be seeing the family again. Naturally, he wanted to go to the station at St. Lazare and wave them off on their train to catch their ship in Normandy.

However, he was forbidden to do so and told to work on the farm whilst Madame Gorse and her three children went to visit the Brusson family in their hotel near the station as preparations were being made for the forthcoming journey.

Samuel Binns fumed at what he perceived to be an injustice against him by the Gorse family and in a fit of temper, he went to the milliner's shop and picked up a measuring iron ring-weight of 20 kilogrammes. When asked by signs by the assistants in the shop where he was going with the heavy iron weight, he responded by signs that he was going to use it to break his aunt's head when she returned home from visiting the Brusson family.

The shop assistants were able to get word to Madame Gorse to take precautions and were also able to prevent Binns from carrying out his threat by relieving him of the iron weight. Binns was banished to the farm by an angry Madame Gorse with instructions to the other staff to keep him on the farm the next day whilst she went to the station with her children to see off

Gare Saint Lazare station in the 1890s.
It was here that Samuel Binns lay in wait for Madame Gorse

the Brusson family. However, Binns slipped away from the people watching over him and disappeared.

At 8 pm on the evening of Thursday 10th September, whilst Madame Gorse and her three children were saying their good-byes to the Brusson family on the train platform, they were suddenly confronted by Samuel Binns, his face contorted in rage.

Somehow, he had managed to find a revolver from somewhere, and now he pointed it in the direction of Madame Gorse and fired. Never having held a gun before, Binns' aim was poor and the bullet flew harmlessly past Madame Gorse's head. Almost immediately, a second shot was fired followed by a terrible cry. The eldest daughter clutched her breast and slowly fell down on the platform. Binns stared at the fallen girl aghast - he had never meant to hurt the girl.

Before he could raise the gun and fire again at Madame Gorse, Binns was set upon by several people who had witnessed the shooting, and after a struggle, disarmed and handed over to the police.

At his trial, the court was sympathetic to Binns for the abuse he had endured at the hands of Madame Gorse and committed to be held at the state's nearest asylum for the mentally insane.

Stabbed in the chest, *Dublin, Ireland 1899*

Thomas Monahan was a Deaf shoemaker, a trade he had learnt at school, like many others of his generation who went through a deaf education in the late 1890s (and for years afterwards). He could, however, speak quite intelligibly, and people were able to understand him although he tended to shout because he had no means of controlling his voice.

He had lived for a number of years at 9 Thomas Street, Ringsend, Dublin with Mary Ann Martin who was legally married to another man, and who had been in Australia for more than ten years. Monahan and Martin regarded themselves as husband and wife, but in the summer of 1899, Monahan lost his job because of his drinking, and Mary Ann Martin had enough of his drunken abuses, so she told him to leave her house.

However, Monahan continued to visit the house every day until mid-November 1899, when Mrs. Martin told him to stop bothering her as she had a new lover sharing her bed.

There was only one main room in the house, and all the occupants who included Martin's nephews, William Longmore and two much younger boys, slept in the same room, all the boys sharing one bed.

On Saturday night 2 December 1899, Monahan drank heavily as was his custom, and decided that he would pay a visit to Mrs. Martin to try for a reconciliation, but she was having none of it.

As they argued loudly, they woke up the three boys in the room who then witnessed Monahan draw out a shoemaker's knife that he habitually carried, and thrust it at Mary Ann Martin twice. As Martin fell to the floor dying, Monahan dropped the knife and ran out of the house chased by William Longmore, who then ran to a nearby pub and was able to call the police.

A Sergeant Flynn and an Inspector Byrne responded to the call and arranged for Mrs. Martin to be taken to the nearest hospital where she later died of

19

her wounds. She had been stabbed once in the abdomen and once in the chest. She had put her hand out to defend herself and got her right thumb cut off in the process.

The next day, Sergeant Flynn arrested Thomas Monahan who was hiding in a house nearby. The local priest, Father Massey, led the officer to the hiding place after being informed where the fugitive was.

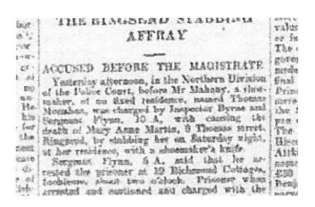

Sent by the magistrates to Dublin Assizes, Thomas Monahan was found guilty of manslaughter and sentenced to a 15-year jail term.

A Case of Patricide , *New Zealand, 1909*

Thomas Nye was a farmer with an eye for the ladies. He was a man of fine physique and popular in the farming community of Foxton in the North island of New Zealand, about 30 kilometres south-west of the main town of Palmerston North. Popular especially at the dances which were regularly held in the district where his attraction to other ladies had been the cause of his divorce to his first wife, who was Deaf. He had three children with her. The eldest, a son named Thomas Hedley, and older daughter Violet, chose to live with their father when he remarried. The youngest, aged 3 at the time of the divorce, chose to live with the mother who had remarried and now lived in Wellington.

Thomas Nye himself did not remain unattached for long. He soon married a woman named Agnes Burston who was also divorced, with a son named Lionel.

The boy, called Hedley rather than his first given name, was found to be Deaf and sent away to the Sumner School for Deaf Mutes, in Christchurch where he remained for seven years, rarely coming home.

Institution for the Deaf and Dumb, Sumner, Christchurch
Hedley Nye, along with his Deaf mother and younger Deaf sister,
attended this school

Whilst at the school. Hedley Nye was regarded as an exemplary pupil who did well in his studies, and was a particular favourite of his teacher, Gerrit Van Asch. He learnt to produce some understandable speech and was a top athlete at the school in his final year.

However, after leaving the school in 1904, his mental capacity deteriorated and he was unable to hold down a regular job. This may have been due to lack of contact with other Deaf people he could communicate with. He was also disinclined to do any work on his father's farm, going absent several times and on occasion turning up at his real mother's residence in Wellington. Perhaps he felt more at ease in his mother's Deaf household where all communication was in sign language. However, his mother and new husband declined to accept responsibility for the boy so he was sent back to his father.

Moody and at times unsociable, he hung around the farm becoming at times a nuisance and strain to his father and stepmother. He was heard (and seen by his signs) several times to utter threats to his father, imitating that he would kill him.

At the farm, Hedley occupied a room on the upper floor of the farmhouse whilst his father and stepmother occupied the main bedroom on the lower floor. His sister Violet and stepbrother Lionel occupied two adjoining bedrooms on the upper floor separately from Hedley.

On the night of Sunday 4 July 1909, Hedley retired to his room after supper at 7:30 pm. His parents did not retire until 10:30 pm, and the other two children shortly afterwards. However, the parents were unable to sleep on the lower floor as they were continually disturbed by Hedley walking about in his room. The footfalls were particularly heavy at times, but neither parent desired to go up and quieten the young man, for fear of setting off a temper or tantrum.

However, at about 1 am, both parents heard Hedley walking noisily down the stairs, and telling his wife to remain in bed, the father got out of bed and went out of the room to see what was the reason for his son coming downstairs. He was mindful of the fact that Hedley had run away on several occasions in the past, and had no wish for a similar occurrence to happen again.

Thomas Nye

Suddenly, there was a loud roar and Agnes Nye shot out of bed alarmed. Running out of her room, she was confronted by the body of her husband lying at the foot of the stairs, and the sight of her stepson holding a double-barrelled shotgun. As she screamed her husband's name, the boy brushed past her and went to the kitchen, opening drawers to search for more bullets.

Meanwhile, Lionel Burston had been shaken out of his sleep by the commotion and had run downstairs to see what the matter was, and had tripped over his stepfather's body in the hallway. He screamed at his stepsister Violet to hide and ran out of the house to avoid his stepbrother.

Meanwhile, Agnes Nye spotted Hedley coming out of the kitchen reloading the shotgun, and also ran out of the house, chased by Hedley who lost her in the darkness among the bushes. Agnes Nye did not stop running until she reached a neighbouring homestead and raised the alarm. Police responding to the call found Violet Nye hiding in a locked and bolted room, and Lionel Burston hiding in the bush.

There was no sign of Hedley Nye, who was somewhere loose in the night outside the house with the shotgun. The police put out a search for him, warning other residents in the area that Hedley was armed and dangerous, and there were reports that he had been seen heading in the direction of Levin, presumably trying to go and see his mother.

One of the searching officers, Constable Beagrie, was informed that the fugitive had been spotted at Levin railway station, and approached him cautiously. However, Hedley made no resistance as the police officer took the gun away from him. The constable wrote on a slip of paper, "You are charged with murder."

The boy wrote back, "Yes." He was then taken back to Foxton where an inquest heard evidence from Agnes Nye and several police officers.

Mrs. Nye stated that upon hearing the shot, she had come out of the room and seen Hedley in the kitchen searching through drawers. She had run out of the front door but did not go out of the grounds. She had hidden behind a fir tree until she had seen Hedley go back into the house after giving up looking for her. She had screamed at Lionel and Violet to hide, then run to her neighbour Mr. Symons' house to raise the alarm. She stated that Hedley had several times threatened to kill his father, but they had thought nothing of it. She added that there had been no quarrel or arguments of any sort before Hedley went up to bed that evening.

When Hedley Nye was brought before the coroner, it seemed to observers that he did not fully realise the predicament he was in, smiling at people and laughing to himself at times. The coroner and court officials were at a loss how to swear him in or to communicate with him.

An uncle was asked to sit alongside the youth and upon the coroner's directions, wrote:

"Do you understand what an oath means?"

The youth wrote underneath: *"Yes."*

The next question was: *"Will you swear to tell the truth?"*

There was a smile when the youth wrote: *"I do not think of it."*

The uncle then wrote: *"Do you know your father is dead?"*

There was another smile as he nodded and wrote: *"Yes"*

When the coroner asked the uncle to write: *"Do you know how he died?"*, the court-appointed solicitor for Hedley Nye stopped the questioning saying that the youth should not answer any questions that incriminated himself.

The coroner then announced his verdict which was written down for the boy's benefit: *"That Thomas Nye came by his death from a gunshot wound inflicted by his son, Hedley Nye."*

It was decided to show the verdict to the accused, who read it carefully more than once, then picking up a pencil, wrote: *"That Thomas Nye sends the thank you."*

Hedley Nye came up before the Foxton Police Court on Monday 12 July where more evidence was presented. On this occasion, the court managed to obtain the services of an interpreter, a Mrs. Stewart whose experience and competence was not questioned.

Hedley was represented by a defence solicitor, a Mr. Dix, who informed the court before any evidence had been submitted that he wished to raise a complaint about the conduct of the gaoler at Palmerston North jail. The complaint was that he had been prevented from having a confidential session with the prisoner in order that the prisoner's views of the shooting incident could be ascertained in order to formulate and present a defence.

Counsel for the police apologised for this incident and undertook that there would be no further occurrence of the accused being denied his legal rights to privacy with his legal representatives.

Evidence was given by a Dr. Adams who was called to the house at 2:30 am accompanied by Constable Woods. Approaching the house, the doctor said that they were met with screams of someone calling out "Father." He and Constable Woods had entered the house by the front door. The house was in darkness but immediately in front of them, they could see the body of a man lying in the doorway of the dining room with his head towards them. He was lying on his back with his head in a large pool of blood. There was a large gunshot wound on the side of his neck. He had fallen straight down and there was a candle and a box of matches on the body. They had searched the rest of the house and found hiding in one of the rooms the deceased's daughter, Violet Nye, whose screams of help they had heard. There was no sign of the gunman, who they now knew to be Hedley Nye, in the house, but in the garden, they found hiding and shivering the son of Mrs. Nye, Lionel Burston.

Dr. Adams stated that the post-mortem showed a large gunshot wound the size of a man's palm on the left side of the neck which had shattered the lower left jaw and severed the artery and jugular veins. Death had been instantaneous.

The widow Agnes Nye told the court that on the Thursday preceding the tragedy, she has seen Hedley in the kitchen and when she asked what he was doing, he pushed her away , gathered everything up and ran outside. She had not realised until afterwards that what she had seen were cartridges, and upon searching Hedley's jacket after he had gone to bed, she found five cartridges in one of the pockets and gave them to her husband. After this incident, no cartridges were kept in the kitchen.

Hedley Nye did not give any evidence and his lawyer pled not guilty for him on his behalf, and reserved his defence as the accused was committed for trial to the next Supreme Court sitting.

The scene was therefore set for the Supreme Court sitting at Palmerston North on Monday August 23 1909. Presiding was Judge Cooper, and Hedley's defence counsel was a Mr. Wilford, whilst Mr. C. A. Loughnan appeared for the Crown.

Hedley Nye was charged with one count of murder, but an alternative charge of manslaughter was also preferred.

Mr. Wilford drew the attention of the court to a similar case that had happened in England and asked that three issues be resolved, namely:

1.   Whether the accused was a mute by malice or by the visitation of

God;

2.   Whether he was able to plead; and

3.   Whether he was sane or not.

Evidence was then called to show that Hedley Nye had been a deaf-mute all his life. His uncle, Archibald Osborne, deposed that he had known the youth all his life and he had never been anything other than a deaf-mute. He had gone away to the Institution at Sumner where he had been taught some speech, but since he had left school, the youth had forgotten how to speak properly.

Joseph Edward Stevens, who was headmaster of the school, testified that Hedley Nye was accepted into the school on 9 February 1897, and had left the school in the summer of 1904. When Hedley had left school, he had some understandable speech, but when Mr. Stevens examined him before the trial, he found that the boy's intelligible speech had deteriorated and that his mental capacity was markedly impaired compared to what he was while at school.

The High Court at Palmerston North where Hedley Nye was tried.

The next proceeding was to decide if the accused was fit to plead. Again, without retiring, the jury returned a verdict that the accused was a lunatic and so was unable to plead.

The judge then committed Hedley Nye to the Porirua Mental Asylum during the pleasure of the Minister for Internal Affairs.

It is not known whether Hedley Nye was ever released from the Mental Asylum but he died in Porirua on 16 May 1977 and was buried in Porirua Cemetery.

Hedley Nye's gravestone in Porirua Cemetery.

Double Murder-Suicide, *England 1914*

In August 1914, the whole world was staring into an abyss which would affect the lives of millions of people. Earlier in June, the heir to the throne of Austria-Hungary, Archduke Franz Ferdinand was assassinated by a Yugoslav nationalist in Sarajevo, Serbia which subsequently led to Austria declaring war on Serbia on 28 July.

This was followed on 1 August by Germany declaring war on Russia, and on 3 August also declaring war on France and simultaneously invading Belgium. This forced Britain, which had pledged support to Belgium, to declare war on Germany.

At that time, no-one really thought how disastrous these events would turn out for most of the world and many events continued as if peace still existed, with sporting events still being in the news, family and community life carrying on as usual, whether good or bad. This was certainly true of life among Deaf people in Britain.

In the space of a few days, two tragedies took place one hundred miles apart when two men committed identical crimes. The first took place on Monday night 10 August at Fazakerley, Liverpool when a Deaf man named William Holden, aged 30, accosted a Deaf woman named Ethel Amelia Frost, aged 24.

They had previously been going out together for two years but the previous Friday, the girl had told Holden that she no longer wished to see him, as she had now taken up with another young Deaf man, Joseph Brindley Jones.

Both men had a confrontation in the house of another Deaf woman, Jessie Hellier on the Monday afternoon, and Hellier had told Holden to get out of her house. Holden told Frost that he was going away for good, and she said that she was glad to be rid of him.

However, Holden lay in wait for Frost to leave her friend's house and they went for a walk along Queens Drive before the young girl returned to her friend's house saying that she was finding it difficult to get rid of Holden and had arranged to meet him again that night.

The next morning, their bodies were discovered at the back of Everton Cemetery. Both their throats were cut. There had evidently been a struggle, and a razor was found near Holden's body. It was clear the wounds had been inflicted whilst they were standing up.

In giving evidence at the inquest via an interpreter, Jessie Hellier said that Holden had been possessively jealous, and though the couple had announced their plans to marry, Ethel Frost had grown weary of Holden's jealousy and had sought to break it off several times. Holden had once thrown himself under a car, which had stopped just in time, and had threatened more than once to shoot Frost, her new boyfriend, then himself.

The inquest was told that several rambling letters had been found in Holden's coat pocket and also in Frost's satchel, the content showing that Holden had no control over his mind or his pen.

The jury returned a verdict that stated Holden had murdered Ethel Amelia Frost whilst temporarily insane and committed suicide.

Meanwhile, three days after Holden had killed Frost then himself, an almost identical crime was being committed in Mansfield, Nottinghamshire.

Three young men were walking on the main road near the recreation ground just before 11 pm when they noticed a couple in animated argument under the shadow of some trees a little way off. Suddenly, the woman broke away from the man and rushed up to the group and flung her arms around one of them named Bingley who found himself covered in blood. As he lay her down on the road, the man with whom she had been arguing came up and before the three young men could interfere, he bent down and cut the woman's throat with a razor, then just as quickly, he pulled the razor across his own throat.

Although a doctor was quickly on the scene, the man's injuries were so severe that he died on the way to hospital.

DOUBLE TRAGEDY.
HUSBAND MURDERS WIFE.

TWENTY years of unhappy married life were brought to a sudden termination by a double tragedy. While three young men were talking in the main Nottingham road, Mansfield, England, just before 11 p.m., they noticed a couple meet under the shadow of some trees near the recreation ground Suddenly the woman rushed up to the group and put her arms around the neck of one. She had evidently been

Newspaper reports of the two murder-suicides in the same week.

The coroner's inquest heard that Samuel Slater, 45, and his 36-year-old wife had twenty years of an unhappy married life punctuated by regular fights and arguments, although the marriage produced three children.

In May, Mrs. Slater had sought a separation order on the grounds of her husband's cruelty. She told the family court through sign language interpreters that on 18 April her husband broke a lamp in the house, as well as thrashing it completely, nearly setting fire to the property. The wife alleged that he was not fit to live with and that on one occasion, he had tried to strangle her. Through the 20 years of married life, he had made things uncomfortable for her. In his defence, the husband asserted he had no wish to be at cross-purposes with her, and that it was merely too much Easter ale that upset him. The wife, however, refused to go back to him and the separation order was granted.

The husband refused to comply with the separation order and Mrs Slater had him arrested on a warrant, following which Slater was committed to prison for a short sentence. At the time of his sentencing, he had threatened in signs to "do" his wife.

Samuel Slater had only just come out of prison when he waylaid his wife in the recreation ground as she was returning home from a night out, and carried out his threat.

The coroner's jury returned a verdict of murder and *felo de se*, an archaic legal term meaning suicide. In early English common law, an adult who committed suicide was literally a felon, and the crime was punishable by forfeiture of property to the Crown and given a shameful burial where no mourners or clergy was present.

Deaf Cannibal Gipsies, *Slovakia 1929*

On 5 November 2011, Slovak police, acting on a tip-off, arranged to have an undercover officer impersonate a Swiss national who had agreed to become a victim of a cannibal. The would-be victim later changed his mind and went to the police upon learning that the man he was to meet had stated he had just killed and eaten two Slovak women.

The would-be cannibal realised that the man he was to meet in a forest near Kosice, Slovakia, was not who he said he was during Internet conversations prior to the meeting, and sensing that he was part of a police undercover operation, he opened fire on the undercover police officer. In the gun battle that followed with police officers supporting their undercover officer, the would-be cannibal was hit several times and arrested as he lay wounded on the ground before being rushed to hospital together with one police officer who had been hit in the gun battle.

The 43-year-old suspect, a father of two young daughters, had used the Internet to search for people willing to commit suicide and let him eat their bodies. The Swiss national later got 'cold feet' when he realised the enormity of what he was letting himself in for.

After the suspect and the police officer had been rushed to hospital in separate ambulances, police raided his house where they uncovered evidence of past cannibalism and also future plans to lure more victims to satisfy his depraved tastes. Some of the evidence uncovered suggested that not only did the suspect murder and eat two Slovak woman, 20-year-old Lucia Uchnarova and Elena Gudjakova, but that he had also targeted some Italian women as well.

The day after the gun battle, the would-be cannibal died in hospital of his wounds and was named as Matej Curko *(below)*

Astonishingly, this was not the first case of cannibalism in the Kosice province of Slovakia. Cannibalism had been practised in the region as far back as people could remember, mostly by the poor Roma Gipsy population that resided in the forests and other rural and hard to reach locations around Kosice.

A typical Roma Gipsy family from Slovakia, 1925

In 1924, there was a trial in Szepsi, Slovakia (a town not far from Kosice) involving a large number of gipsies accused of cannibalism. However, as cannibalism was not part of the Czechoslovak Criminal Code, they were all found not guilty and released, especially as no remains of any bodies could be found.

In 1929, nineteen of the same group, including two women, were arrested for further cannibalistic activities. This time however, they faced charged of murder because some remains, including that of a young boy, were found and linked to the group. The authorities found the proceedings of the trial exceedingly difficult to manage, not because of the differences in Roma language and the Czech language, but also because the majority of those arrested were Deaf without any form of speech, or in deed education. They were not only illiterate but also incapable of understanding the nature of their "crimes". To them, cannibalism was just a form of eating to survive. Many of the "witnesses" in the trial were also uneducated Deaf gipsies.

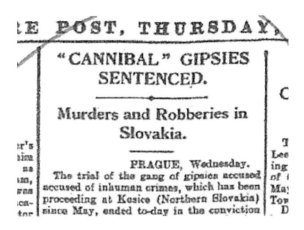

The leader of the Roma group, Alexander Filke, was found guilty and sentenced to 25 years penal servitude. Other members of the group were also found guilty or conspiracy to murder and sentenced to between 8 and 15 years each in prison although some were released because charges against them could not be proved.

A sick wife murdered, *Mitcham, Surrey, England 1932*

When a neighbour heard knocking sounds followed after a minute by a thud from the house next door at 3 o'clock in the early morning of Tuesday 9 August 1932, the husband got out of bed to go and look out of his window but could not see anything, so returned to bed. He knew that the people who lived next door were both Deaf and sometimes made noises without realising they were doing so. He also knew that the wife, Sophia Carrett, had been ill for several years and an invalid since 1928, going in and out of hospital several times.

John William Carrett, the husband who was at age 56 five years younger than his wife, had been depressed about his wife's health for some weeks. Only two days previously, he had asked Sophia Carrett's brother and sister-in-law, Mr. & Mrs. Robinson who were both also Deaf, to stay at his house to provide more care to his wife, and they were sleeping in an upstairs room at the time. They were disturbed at 6 a.m. by John Garrett coming into the bedroom they were sleeping in, and taking from a wardrobe some clothes which he took out onto the landing and got dressed there. When Mr. Robinson followed him out of the bedroom, he found that John Carrett was dressed in his best clothes and ready to go out of the house. He also had his hat on. He was looking very ill.

Mr. Robinson signed, "I thought you were going to work?"

Carrett signed back, "Will never work again in my life." He then exited the house.

Mrs Robinson, who had followed her husband downstairs, tried the door handle of the room which Mrs. Carrett was using, and found it locked. Climbing on the window sill, she saw Mrs. Carrett lying on a couch. She appeared to be dead, and a milkman heard Mrs. Robinson's screams and sent for the police.

When the police arrived, they summoned a doctor before breaking the door to get into the room.

They found Mrs. Carrett dead with a pair of braces pulled tightly around her throat and the doctor stated she had been dead at least a couple of hours. In addition to the braces around her neck, there were cuts on the neck, and cuts and bruises on the face, chin, chest, arms and on one leg. There was also a broken penknife on the mantelpiece.

Police recovered a rambling note that was lying on Mrs. Carrett's body, which said:

> Get all you can and take this lot to Nellie Bicknell and Harry Bicknell. You told me lies Nell: her age 62. She thought it was Alf. I hope you enjoy money from insurance. £20 if you lucky. My hand very bad. I had lot of work to do. Told you before what I would do so all the world will know.

It transpired that the Harry Bicknell referred to was the son from Mrs. Carrett's first marriage, and Nellie was his wife.

The inquest into Mrs. Carrett's death learnt that on 5 August, Mrs. Carrett was unusually ill and the next day, 6 August, John Carrett had called upon the Bicknell house in nearby Sutton and asked them to go and see Mrs. Carrett as she did not have long to live. John Carrett appeared morose and bad-tempered, and was unusually strange in his manner, complaining of pains in his head. He had handed over to Harry Bicknell the sum of £20 saying that this was half of his mother's money and that he would get the other half after her death. He had then grabbed Nellie Bicknell by the arms and kissed her so suddenly and forcibly on the lips that her teeth cut one of her lips. John Carrett had then said, "I love you like daughter now."

Mrs. Bicknell told police that her stepfather-in-law had been very devoted in his care of her mother-in-law during her illness and had been under considerable strain.

Meanwhile, there was no trace of John Carrett in the locality of Mitcham and Sutton, although it was discovered later he had gone to the home of a Deaf friend, Mrs. Lockyer, spending some hours there and showing her some jewellery and a swollen hand. Mrs. Lockyer told a later court hearing that Carrett had been in a strange and distressed condition which she put down to his being stressed out by his wife's illness.

Unobserved by police, Carrett had made his way back to his house which was supposed to be under guard, and had pushed another note through an open window which said:

Nothing to be taken from this house, by my order. J. W. Carrett.

Needless to say, the inspector in charge of the murder investigation was not impressed by the lack of security of the murder scene.

However, in the early hours of the morning of Wednesday 10 August, an unkempt and dishevelled man appeared before Police-Sergeant Cecil Goffe and said, "I am Mr. Carrett. I want to give myself up for murder."

Goffe said that Carrett appeared to be very tired and there was a dazed and vacant look in his eyes.

Later, when he was charged with murder, he had made a second brief statement, "I cannot make no other statement. It is murder as far as I understand it."

He made a brief appearance at Croydon Petty Sessions later that afternoon charging with wilfully murdering his wife, Sophia Carrett.

How the arrest and the court appearance was reported in the local newspapers.

John Carrett appeared again at Croydon Petty Sessions on Thursday 18 August when he pleaded not guilty and was remanded in custody to be tried at the Central Criminal Court (Old Bailey) at its next sessions, which subsequently heard that Carrett had been under increasing strain over his wife's deteriorating health and had been devoted in his care of her until he could take no more. He had then tried to hasten her death by strangling her with braces, and hitting her in the face.

The jury at the Old Bailey trial returned a verdict saying that Carrett had killed whilst the balance of his mind was disturbed with grief over his wife's pending death.

He was sentenced to be retained during His Majesty's Pleasure in a mental institution. It is not known if he was later released.

"Johnny Belinda", *Prince Edward Island, Canada, c1880 & 1948*

A film with Jane Wyman in the lead role was produced in 1948 and received such acclaim that Wyman received her first Oscar for her performance in that lead role. The unusual thing was that for the first time since the era of silent movies, the Oscar was given to someone who never spoke one word throughout the film.

The film, *Johnny Belinda,* was adapted by a play by Elmer Blaney Harris and based on the allegedly true story of a deaf and dumb girl growing up on a farm in Prince Edward Island, Canada. Harris was an American playwright working out of New York and San Francisco (until the earthquake of 1906 destroyed his newspaper offices and studio, after which he was based mainly in New York where he married in 1908).

After his marriage, he built a summer residence on Prince Edward Island and he would write three plays later turned into silent films based on the characters and actual people living near his summer home. One of the people he got to know was the Deaf girl, who lived not far from his residence at Fortune Bay. Obviously there were communication difficulties and the girl herself was bit of a recluse, and it is not certain that he even got the full story, as the play/film deviates from the truth in several instances - it also relocates the scene from Prince Edward Island to Cape Breton.

What he wrote was about the Deaf girl named Belinda, living in a small fishing village with her father and her aunt, her mother having dies in childbirth. She can not communicate with her family and lives in a world all her own. Until, a doctor named Robert, comes to help the family with the birth of a calf. He and Belinda quickly become friends and he teaches her sign language.

One evening, one of the farm customers named Locky McCormick and his girl friend, Stella Maguire, stop by the farm with a group of their friends. They begin playing music and dancing and Robert places Belinda's hand on a violin so that she can feel music for the first time.

Later that night, having been rejected by Stella, a drunken Locky rapes Belinda, who is on her own at the farm. Belinda becomes withdrawn and her father asks Robert to find out what is wrong with her. Robert takes Belinda to town to visit an ear specialist and learns that she is pregnant. Robert only tells Aggie, knowing her   father will take it hard.

One Sunday her father and Robert take her to church for the first time. Locky and Stella also attend the service and Belinda's reaction to Locky made Robert think that he may be the father of the child.

After the baby is born the townspeople, believing that Robert is the child's father, ostracize him and Belinda's family. Robert offers to marry Belinda, but her father does not think it is a very good idea because he is not in love with her. However, Robert leaves town to start a new practice and promises to send for Belinda as soon as he can.

While he is away, Locky with his new wife Stella show up during a storm. Belinda's father suddenly realizes the identity of his grandson's father and the two men get into a fight and Locky pushes the father off a cliff to his death.

Locky urges the townspeople to declare Belinda unfit to care for the child then turns up at the farm to take the baby away from Belinda. Stella cannot go through with it. Locky then tells Stella that he is the baby's father. But Belinda will not give up the baby without a fight and blocks his path but he shoves her down the stairs. Before he can get to the baby, Belinda grabs a shotgun and kills him. She is then arrested and tried for murder. The doctor returns and testifies at Belinda's trial that she was only protecting her property and her family.

The court, still under the belief that he is the baby's father, dismisses his evidence, but Locky's widow, Stella, corroborates the doctor's story and testifies that her   husband had confessed the truth about the rape, and that he was the baby's true father, and that he had killed Belinda's father by pushing him off a cliff during their fight.

Jane Wyman as Belinda in the film.

The rape as depicted in the film

Belinda is then set free.

BUT...

How close to the truth was the play and film as written by Elmer Blaney Harris? We already know that the location had changed to Cape Breton but what other differences are there? These differences are:

- The real identity of the girl was Lydia Dingwell (1852-1931), born to Joseph (Red Joe) and Zipporah (nee Mills) Dingwell.

- Joseph Dingwell (the father) died of old age in 1908, therefore was not pushed off a cliff.

- Zipporah Dingwell died of old age in 1910, and not - as stated in the play/film - in childbirth.

- The trial of Lydia Dingwell did not happen.

- The film is set in 1946-1948, not around 1880.

What is fact is:

* Lydia Dingwell never married, but had three children: William (born 1882); Alonzo (both 1884); Laura May (born 1892).

* The rape happened. What is unclear is which child was the product of the rape.

* Lydia Dingwell WAS arrested for murder, but the case was dismissed before it came to trial.

Lydia Dingwell is interred (buried) beside her parents Joseph and Zipporah Dingwell in an unmarked grave at Dingwells Mills, Fortune Bay, Prince Edward Island. This is not far from the former summer residence of Elmer Blaney Harris, which still stands. However, a road now goes through the old Dingwell farm.

Blame the interpreter! *New York, 1985 & 2012*

New York 1985.

Two Deaf gangs moved around the Bronx in 1985, sometimes crossing paths which led to violence. Sometimes the gangs shared or used the same girls (also Deaf). Sometimes individual members of the gangs carried guns, but mostly they used knives to threaten and scare people.

Miguel Lopez belonged to the gang called the Outside Boys. Ordinarily, this gang would not hang about the East 190th Street area in Bronx, which was regarded as the territory of their rival gang, the Crazy Homicides. Members of this gang included Steven Torres, George Magriz, Eddie Velasquez, Gabriel Thompson and Hernando ('Henry') Lopez - no relation to Miguel Lopez.

However, there was a crack-house at 1013 E. 190th Street which supplied both gangs, and Miguel Lopez went there on 31 August 1985 to obtain some crack for some of his gang members, and as luck would have it, he was spotted by the 5 members of the Crazy Homicides. There were other members of the gang hanging around near the crack-house, just watching.

Henry Lopez was particularly annoyed with Miguel Lopez because he had heard Miguel was shagging his girlfriend, Lillian Gonzales and wanted to confront him to warn him off.

This was nothing new. Eight months previously, Gabriel Thompson had a confrontation himself with Miguel Lopez over the fact he believed Lopez had infected Thompson's girlfriend of the time, Matilda Ayala, with a sexually transmitted disease which he had passed onto Thompson. The confrontation took place in Thompson's apartment where there was a birthday party going on and Miguel Lopez turned up uninvited to argue about the "possession" of Matilda Ayala. During the confrontation, Lopez's hand had gone behind to the small of his back and re-appeared with a gun in his hand. Despite the implied threat, Thompson had stood his ground and told Miguel Lopez to get out of his apartment.

Thus, when Henry Lopez went to confront his namesake Miguel on the sidewalk outside the crack-house, Gabriel Thompson watched Miguel's reactions closely, and sure enough, his right hand went behind his back in the same way it had during the earlier confrontation. This time, however, Eddie Velasquez had gone round behind Lopez and pinioned him whilst Thompson slid a knife into Miguel Lopez's chest. All this had taken a split second and everyone watching was uncertain as to what exactly had happened.

As Miguel Lopez fell dying onto the sidewalk, the Crazy Homicides gang members melted away into the night.

NYPD detectives shrugged the it off as yet another gang-related incident and although some perfunctory enquiries were made during which several names came up, including Thompson's and Velasquez's plus an associate of Miguel Lopez named Al Rodriguez, the case remained unsolved.

Thompson left the neighbourhood in 1986, a year after the murder, when he moved to Washington, D.C. to attend Gallaudet University, where he studied business administration for three months before he had to drop out because his father could not afford to pay his tuition anymore. It was at Gallaudet, that Thompson met Andrea Velez, a woman who would become his wife. Thompson and Velez, who could hear, moved to Queens after Thompson dropped out of Gallaudet. Thompson worked whenever he could, mostly as a mailroom clerk in mid-town Manhattan.

Thompson and Velez were married in 1991. They had four daughters: Maybelle, now 20, Jacqueline, 18, Gladys, 16, and Velancia, 5.

Thompson and Velez separated in 2005 and he moved to Lancaster, Pennsylvania, because a friend told him of a place there where he could stay. In Lancaster, Thompson said he first worked in the cleaning service at a hospital but didn't like it. He quit and began doing odd jobs through Labor Ready, an agency which supplied temporary workers. In 2007, Thompson and Velez divorced.

In the meantime, the unsolved killing of Miguel Lopez had been turned over to the NYPD's Cold Case squad. However, this squad consisted of only three men and their caseload ran into the hundreds, so there was only so much they could do, and relied mainly on tips coming into the squad room.

Detective Padilla, one of the three men in the squad, got a call from a woman named Janet Ortiz who said that her boyfriend, Nathaniel Russell, who was an old friend of Thompson told her that his friend had sort of brought up the Lopez murder, hinting that he had been involved.

Reviewing the old case files, Padilla found that the original detectives investigating the stabbing of Miguel Lopez did not find the murder weapon, and that witnesses interviewed at the time said they had not recognised the killer.

Padilla ran Thompson's name through several databases and found that he did not have a criminal record. However, he had the feeling that Janet Ortiz's tip was worth following up. There was the danger that there were personal issues involved because Thompson and Russell had fallen out because Thompson had tried to bed Ortiz, and he decided to re-interview some of the original witnesses, one of whom was Al Rodriguez.

"I read his account from back in 1985," said Padilla. "And I just had a hunch, man, that he knew who the killer was."

Padilla tracked Rodriguez down in upstate New York and went to see him. "One of my first questions was, 'Do you know who killed your friend?'" he said. Rodriguez told Padilla that Gabriel Thompson had done it.

"If I move too fast without getting all my evidence together, then I'm wasting my time," said Padilla. He said The Bronx Cold Case Squad only had three people at the time so he was working on several cases at once and could not devote all his efforts to finding Thompson.

Padilla said that over the next few years, several people from the Bronx Deaf community called him with new information about the case and that in 2010 he got a tip that Thompson was staying with a woman in an apartment at 3285 Rombouts Avenue in the Bronx, a government housing project for deaf people. On September 3, 2010, Padilla went to the brick building where the superintendent showed him a guest log in which Thompson's name appeared. The superintendent told Padilla that Thompson drove a black Dodge Durango with Pennsylvania license plates that was parked around the corner.

Padilla decided to "sit on the car" until Thompson showed up, which meant he "sat in an unmarked car, drank coffee, and ate doughnuts for as long as it took."

Thompson showed up that same afternoon with Oscar Marcelino, the boyfriend at the time of Angie Acevedo, the woman with whom Thompson was staying. "[Gabriel] was just quiet, standing there with my ex-boyfriend fixing a car," wrote Acevedo, who was also Deaf. "Then a cop came to see [Gabriel].... He didn't know what happened. Police said, 'Come in car.'"

A woman named Wendy Duarte, who also lived in the building, served as an interpreter between Padilla and Thompson at the housing project. Padilla asked Thompson if he would be willing to come in for questioning and Thompson said yes. Padilla later testified before a grand jury that if Thompson had refused to go, he would not have arrested him and that would have probably been the end of it.

Marcelino decided to go with Thompson and they both got in the backseat of Padilla's car. Padilla sat in the front seat and his partner drove. The car was originally headed to the 52nd Precinct, but after Padilla found out there was no sign language interpreter at headquarters, he decided to go to the 109th precinct in Queens, where Police Officer Julio Vasquez, who was married to a Deaf woman and was fluent in sign language was based.

On arrival at the precinct station, Thompson had a cup of coffee while he was asked general questions about his health and education, which, through Vasquez, he answered cooperatively. Padilla did not want to ask straightaway if Thompson had killed a person in case he got defensive.

Padilla then asked Thompson about the events of August 31, 1985, and then at 9:24 p.m., almost an hour and a half after the interrogation began, Thompson told him that he had stabbed Lopez. The questioning was stopped for four minutes, during which time Thompson had a cigarette and Padilla figured out how to read a deaf man his Miranda rights.

Vasquez told Thompson his rights in sign language and then Thompson signed a written version of them.

Thompson began working on a written statement summarising what he had told detectives at 10:05 p.m. He was later taken to Bronx Central Booking where he recorded a video statement and was read his rights again on camera in sign language.

Gabriel Thompson during his video-taped confession which he later wanted thrown out because he claimed he was misled by his interpreter, a police officer.

There should have, he said, been a properly independent qualified interpreter present in the station.

Based on this video confession, Thompson was charged with murder in the second degree and faced a minimum sentence of 15 years to life and a maximum of 25 years to life. Later, his defence attorney tried to get Thompson's confession dismissed, claiming there were "questions of thoroughness" concerning Vasquez's sign language, particularly a couple of instances in which Vasquez did not know the signs for certain words and Thompson had to teach them to him.

According to court transcripts, Vasquez said he knew sign language because his wife was deaf and he had been signing with her for about 18 years. The defence attorney said there were moments in the interrogation video where there was a lot more signing than talking, but, according to Assistant District Attorney Meredith Holtzman, the prosecutor in the case, when another interpreter looked at the video and made a transcript, it was clear that no important information was lost in translation.

The court decided Thompson's confession would be admitted into evidence because he had been read his rights three times, and so Thompson took a plea deal. Thompson pleaded guilty to manslaughter in the second degree, as opposed to murder, and on September 27, 2012, was sentenced to four to 12 years in prison, depending on his behaviour, with no possibility of parole.

He is now (January 2015) serving his time at Eastern Correctional Facility in Napanoch, in Ulster County, New York.

A gang who lived for violence, *Rotterdam, Netherlands 1988*

For three months in the spring of 1988, Dutch police were plagued by the criminal activities of a group of youths, mostly in the Kralingen area of Rotterdam.

As the pattern of violent attacks began to emerge, it seemed to the police that the youths were doing it for nothing more than kicks, and the thrill of targeting strangers.

The first attack actually started at Easter, 1987 with the attack and robbery of a 58-year-old man named Jaap Brasser who was returning home from an evening spent drinking at a bar in the Maas area of Rotterdam. As he returned to his house in the Charlois district by means of the 1370 metre-long Maastunnel, which linked both sides of the Maas River and was well-used by cyclists and pedestrians as well as by vehicles, he was set upon and savagely attacked by a group of youths who knocked him down, gave him multiple kicks in the head and stabbed him in the neck and in the back. The youths then took all the man's money and vanished.

When Brasser was discovered by another passer-by, he was barely alive and taken to hospital, he spent months in a coma therefore unable to assist police in their enquiries as to the perpetrators of the crime.

The next known attack by the gang happened nearly ten months later on 13 February 1988, although police believed there were other attacks in the interim period which were not reported.

On this occasion, a senior municipal officer named Wim van der Woerdt, aged 64 and within a few months of retirement, was set upon in the hallway of the apartment building in which he lived. The attack on him was particularly savage. He was first threatened with a knife by one youth who rifled his pockets for cash, then felled by two others who took turns kicking him mercilessly in the head. Van der Woerdt was also stabbed eight times in the neck and in the back. Van der Woerdt ended up with a partial cleft skull, broken teeth, a prolapsed orbital and ruptured membranes. Only when the victim was in hospital and on the operating table did the surgical team notice that he had also been stabbed through an open mouth and at the back of his throat, severing his vocal cords. This presumably happened when the victim had opened his mouth to call for help.

On the 16 March, 43-year-old Hjalmar Hansen, who was walking with two surgical sticks following a hospital operation, was attacked at a tram stop, and badly beaten. Only the arrival of a tram prevented the attack being carried out too its fullest extent, and Hansen brushed off the requests of tram passengers to call an ambulance and insisted on going home with his injuries. The next day, his mother found him dead at home from his severe injuries, which included a stiletto knife wound in his back that had penetrated his liver. This had not been noticed by the other tram passengers.

One month later, on April 10, a 91-year-old man was assaulted and robbed inside his own house on the Voorscholerlaan, sustaining severe injuries from which he did not fully recover in what remained of his life.

On 16 May, a fit 28-year-old named Ron Duimel was out jogging along the Plaszoom when he was whacked on the head with a hatchet, which sent him sprawling. He then felt hands trying to take his Walkman radio, and despite his serious injury, he fought them off and was able to use his running skills to speed away from the group of attackers.

The gang must have been frustrated by the jogger's escape because barely a week later, on 22 May, they ambushed a 40-year-old nurse, Gerda Stilkenboom, a mother of three, as she was cycling through the Kralingse forest on her way home from work. She was the first known female victim, and again, she was felled by a hatchet striking the side of her head as she cycled along the path. More axe blows rained down on her head as she fell onto the path.

She was also sexually assaulted by the gang, but they were spotted by other people as they fled the scene, enabling the police to get accurate

Above: The Kralingse Pas, a large area of water used for recreational purposes, a haunt of the gang.

Below: A bridge and path in the Kralingse Bos, a 2 square kilometre of forest adjoining the water, where the gang lay in wait for victims.

descriptions of them. As these descriptions matched that given by the jogger Duimel, the police were able to link the assaults to the same group of youths. Additionally, the youths left behind a bicycle which was to lead to their arrest after it was published in the local newspapers.

Information given to the police identified the bicycle as belonging to a teenager Henk Bijvank* (aged 17), who stated he had lent it to a friend Angelo Wies* (aged 18).

Police found that both Henk Bijvank and Angelo Wies were residents in a home for young people, the Don Bosco house in Oostzeedijk, East Rotterdam.

Staff and other residents in the house informed the police that both boys formed a gang which included Henk's brother Johann and two other boys named Mario Schar* (aged 17) and Elton Jong* (aged 18). All five boys were fans of Rambo-type movies and likened themselves to the characters in those films. Henk Bijvank was the acknowledged leader of the group.

All were from broken homes, and one (Angelo Wies) had been an orphan since the age of 2 years and had been in numerous foster homes where the carers found it difficult to control his behaviour.

There was one other difference between Angelo Wies and the others in the group. Angelo was a deaf-mute with serious psychological and communication problems.

Continued on next page…

Footnote:

Henk and Johann Bijvank, Angelo Wies, Mario Schar and Elton Jong are not the real names of the five boys. Dutch law forbids the publication of the surnames of those who come to trial for criminal activities. In all newspaper reports, the five are named Henk B., Johann B., Angelo the W., Mario S., and Elton J.

When the police found the bicycle belonging to Gerda Stilkenboom at the house (one of the boys had taken it in their getaway instead of Henk Bijvank's, a mistake that led to the discovery of the gang), plus a gold ring that belonged to the murdered woman, they knew they had the right perpetrators and arrested them all.

Henk and Johann Bijvank were the first to be questioned, as the police had to retain Angelo Wies in custody until they could get hold of a sign language interpreter. The younger brother freely admitted that they roamed the streets looking for someone to pounce upon, and kick their heads, as well as stab them.

It was through them that the police first found out about the attack on Jaap Brasser in the Maastunnel. He was still in hospital in a coma on a life support machine. (He did not come out of the coma until over 18 months after his attack.)

The brothers admitted the attack on Wim van der Woerdt only because he was able to identify their photographs shown to him by the police.

It was only when they questioned Angelo Wies through the interpreter that they were also able to link the attacks on Hjalmar Hansen (who was found dead at home the next day with a brain haemorrhage) and the elderly 91-year-old in his own apartment.

The group did not admit to any other attacks outside of the five serious assaults (including that on the jogger) and the murder of Gerda Stilkenboom.

At their first hearing before the court in Rotterdam, three of them (the Bijvank brothers, and Angelo Wies) were sent for psychiatric examination at the Pieter Baancentrum, the psychiatric observation clinic of the Department of Justice. No psychiatric evaluation was demanded of Mario Schar, especially as he did not take part in the attack on Gerda Stilkenboom. Although he was present at some of the other attacks, he was judged to have played a modest role.

The fifth boy, Elton Jong, was released on bail as the only evidence linking him with the assaults was his possession of Gerda Stilkenboom's gold ring. He would be tried at a later date for being in possession of stolen property.

The pre-trial hearing also heard criticism from the magistrates and the police about the poor supervision and security of the Don Bosco house in Oostzeedijk. They questioned how the group of boys could get out and roam the streets at all times of the day and night. Angelo Wies, in particular, frequently absconded, sometimes being found in the room of an 18-year-old girl in another foster home with whom he was having a sexual relationship.

Onthutsende geweldsaffaire komt morgen voor rechter

Vier jongens staan terecht voor 'Kralingse-Bosmoord' en vijf andere ernstige misdrijven

Police searching the roadside for clues following the murder of Gerda Stilkenboom

'Ik word koud van uw gruweldaden'

Police stopping and questioning minibus passengers during their investigation of the murder of Gerda Stilkenboom, and *insert,* the bicycle left behind which led to the arrest of the five youths.

During the period between the pre trail hearing and the actual trial starting, there was some discussion with the Ministry of Justice's Criminal Injuries Compensation Fund for the injuries suffered by some of those attacked, especially Jaap Brasser and Wim van der Woerdt who took matters further. Using his position as a senior municipal officer, he made it clear he wanted to see a by-law brought into the city for architects and housing associations to provide better lighting and security in the lobbies of apartment blocks. He said, "My attackers were waiting for me behind the mailboxes in the flathall. These dark corners attract crime. Architects and housing associations should take this into account. Good lighting and the avoidance of blind spots should be an automatism, and to be accounted for in fire regulations." He added he would be in court to see all his attackers sentenced.

The full trial of the four boys took place in the Rotterdam High Court on Thursday 29 December before judge Joop Spanjersberg, with Prosecutor J. Grass demanding lengthy sentences of at least 15 years imprisonment for the group.

At the sentencing phrase on Friday 13 January, the following sentences were handed down:

- 12 years imprisonment for Henk and Johann Bijvank for their part in the murder of Gerda Stilkenboom.

- 12 years imprisonment for Angelo Wies on the same charge.

- 1-8 years imprisonment to be served concurrently for all three for their parts in the sustained attacks of Jaap Brasser, Wim van der Woerdt, Hjalmar Hansen, the 91-year old man, and Ron Duimel.

- 8 years imprisonment for Mario Schar (whose mother was in court and cried out in anguish) for his part in the attacks on Jaap Brasser, Wim van der Woerdt, Hjalmar Hansen and Ron Duimel. He did not take part in the attack on the 91-year-old, nor in the murder of Gerda Stilkenboom.

A roller-coaster relationship ends in murder, *Santa Ana, California, 1987*

When Mary Mendoza chatted to her next door neighbour and friend, Josephine Vinci, over their backyard fence on Sunday 3 May 1987, little did she know it would be the last time she would have a conversation with her.

During that conversation, Mrs. Vinci had fretted over her Deaf daughter Priscilla's relationship with her boyfriend, saying that Priscilla had broken it off that day, and had been hit in the face by the boyfriend. Mrs. Vinci was afraid for her daughter's well-being.

The next evening at 7:30 pm, Mary Mendoza was disturbed by a hammering at her front door. Opening it, she found herself faced with a young woman she recognised as a friend of Priscilla Vinci who had visited occasionally. The friend scribbled furiously on a notepad that she was concerned about Priscilla. She urged Mrs. Mendoza to come and look through a window as she thought there was somebody on the floor.

Alarmed, Mrs. Mendoza hurried round to her neighbour's house followed by Priscilla's friend and tried all doors, which were locked, then peered through a window. She spotted mother and daughter lying side by side on the kitchen floor, in a pool of blood.

Pulling Priscilla's friend with her, she hurried back to her own house and called the police who arrived post haste and set up an incident van in the street outside the house whilst forensic experts carefully went over the scene.

Mrs. Mendoza told police that her neighbour, Josephine Vinci, was 65 years old and had lost her husband, Sam, the previous December. Her daughter, Priscilla, aged 34, had her own residence but visited her mother almost daily. The neighbour told police that she had last seen Mrs. Vinci the previous evening when they had chatted over the backyard fence. Mrs. Mendoza told police how worried her friend and neighbour had been about the relationship between her daughter and a Deaf man named Ronald James Blaney, Jr.

The next day, a man identifying himself as Ronald Blaney, Sr., and the father of Ronald Blaney, Jr., rang the police and said that his son has just contacted him from his mother's home in Prescott, Arizona and had said something about hurting his girlfriend and her mother. He urged police to check out the property at East Cherry Street, Santa Ana.

Police told him they were already at that property investigating a crime, and requested the address of Ronald's mother in Arizona. Shortly afterwards, three Santa Ana police officers, including one fluent in sign language, travelled to Prescott, and accompanied by Prescott police officers, took Ronald James Blaney, Jr. into custody. He was booked into the Yavapai County Jail in Prescott whilst murder charges were being formalised by the Orange County district attorney's office, which would also set up extradition proceedings to return Blaney to California.

Blaney's trial opened at Orange County Superior Court in September 1989, more than two years after the killings.

The Orange County Superior Court in Santa Ana where
Ronald James Blaney, Jr., went on trial for the murder of
Josephine and Priscilla Vinci.

It would be a courtroom filled with sign language for the testimonies. One interpreter would help Blaney, deaf since birth, to understand what would be said in court. Another would be a backup. A third would help Blaney and his lawyer, Deputy Public Defender James S. Egar, talk to each other. The spectators and witnesses, most of them deaf or partially deaf, would also communicate in sign language.

But it would not be the need for signers that made deafness a predominant factor at Blaney's trial. Deafness would also be a key ingredient in his defence.

Blaney faced a possible sentence of life without parole if convicted of murder in the May 4, 1987, stabbing to death of his former girlfriend, Priscilla Vinci, 33, and her mother, Josephine Vinci, 66, at their Santa Ana home.

"I want this jury to understand Ronald Blaney's life as a deaf person," said defence attorney Egar, "how deafness can contribute to mental illness, how it can place someone under stress for a long time and lead to a short fuse."

Blaney, now 32, was unemployed at the time, and Priscilla Vinci, who was also deaf, had broken up with him.

"Theirs was a stormy relationship; a friend of hers called it a roller-coaster ride," Egar said. "But he certainly loved her. And she had loved him."

It was Priscilla Vinci, he said, who had given Blaney the emotional support he needed as he struggled through a computer school. But they also argued a lot, Egar said, and Priscilla's mother got involved. After an incident in which Blaney apparently struck her daughter and chipped her tooth, she wanted them to split up.

Egar did not contest the fact that it was Blaney who drove his car to the Vinci home on Cherry Street about 5 p.m. that day, and stabbed the two women. The mother, stabbed 18 times, died quickly, according to medical reports. But Priscilla, stabbed 24 times, suffered an even more vicious death. Injuries to the area of each of her eyes occurred before she was dead. It was alleged that blood found on a carving knife, a kitchen knife and a fondue fork indicated they might have been used it torture Priscilla during the attack on her. The prosecution stated that the torture inflicted on Priscilla was "gruesome even to the most hardened sensibilities."

Blood splatters in several rooms and defensive wounds on the women's hands showed that they had struggled for their lives, with Priscilla once making it to the door before her death. She was found with multiple stab wounds to her face and wounds to her back. It was alleged that Blaney stabbed her in the back as she lay on the floor clutching a throw rug to her chest to protect herself.

Afterwards, it was alleged that Blaney took a shower in the victims' home and changed his bloody clothes. He also took money from them and their house keys.

The torture and multiple murder allegations could have led to a possible death sentence verdict. But prosecutors said they did not seek the death penalty because they didn't think a jury would return a death sentence for a handicapped person with no criminal record, so they were going for a sentence of life without parole.

Defence Attorney Egar was asking the jurors to find his client not guilty by reason of insanity. But short of winning that, he was seeking some kind of manslaughter verdict.

"He did not take any weapons to the house with him. This act showed all the signs of occurring during the heat of passion," Egar said.

Other evidence presented to the court included Blaney's left footprint found in blood in a bathroom at the house.

A neighbor (Mrs. Mendoza) recognized Blaney's car outside the Vinci home and recalled her surprise because she had been told by Mrs. Vinci that Priscilla had broken up with him. Shortly after the killings, Blaney's father called police to tell them his son was in Arizona, at his mother's home.

The father testified in court that three weeks before the murders, his son became violently upset about the soured romance and about losing his job.

Ronald Blaney Sr. told jurors that his son had come to his apartment upset because "Priscilla wanted a cooling-off period in their relationship, and he couldn't understand it."

"He was confused," the father said. "He was confused about Priscilla; he was confused about the way the hearing world treated the deaf."

His son had worked in the computer field but had been laid off by a tax consultant group. Before that, he had experienced difficulty in keeping a job or getting promotion. In support of this, Deputy Public Defender Egar introduced a letter in which a bank official rejected Blaney, an employee, for a promotion, saying that his deafness made it improbable that he could handle the job.

The court heard that Priscilla Vinci was popular in the local Deaf community where she was an   activist.

Priscilla Vinci, from a college year book

The jury deliberated five days at the end of the four-month trial before bringing in a verdict of murder with torture in the stabbing death of Priscilla Vinci, and of murder in the case of her mother Josephine Vinci. The following week they were to decide if Blaney of Fountain Valley was sane at the time of the killings.

However, jurors were hopelessly deadlocked over the sanity issue, saying they could not decide whether Ronald James Blaney knew what he was doing when he committed the crime. The Superior Court panel, which was charged with assessing Blaney's sanity after convicting him of murder on 3 October, had deliberated a day and a half before announcing that it could not agree.

Foreman Carol Hazelwood, 54, of Irvine, said jurors voted 10 to 2 in favour of finding Blaney sane, but the evidence was so riddled with uncertainty and contradictions that they could not decide.

"We all agreed he had a mental defect," Hazelwood said. "The question was whether it reached the legal definition of insanity." She said the panel's job was thorny because the psychiatrist and psychologist who testified in the sanity phase gave conflicting testimony about Blaney's mental state.

During the sanity phase, Blaney's attorney had presented evidence that his client suffered congenital brain defects because his mother had rubella when he was born and that he was emotionally unstable, as well.

The judge ordered that a second trial be scheduled to decide the sanity issue. But in January 1992, Blaney agreed to drop his insanity plea when the judge agreed to recommend that Blaney be sent to the California Men's Colony at San Luis Obispo, where other deaf and hearing-impaired inmates were housed. There was also a medical facility there where Blaney could be treated for epilepsy.

Ronald James Blaney, Jr., was then sentenced to life without the possibility of parole on March 27 1992.

The Survivor, *Clifton, New Jersey, 1991*

It was the foul smell that drove other occupants in the apartments in the two-storey building at 176 Ackerman Avenue, Clifton, New Jersey to ask the police to investigate, that and the continuous sounds of a baby crying. There was also the fact that the occupants of one of the four apartments in the building had not been seen or heard for over a week, especially "heard" by the other apartment occupants for the apartment where the smell was coming from were occupied by a Deaf family. They can't help it, but Deaf people make more noise than those who can hear. Without really realising it, they allow doors, cupboard doors and drawers to bang shut, rattle crockery more nosily and emanate more noise from their day-to-day activities such as leaving a television on at a high volume if they forgot to put it on mute.

The house at 176 Ackerman Avenue, Clifton, New Jersey to which police were called to investigate reports of a "foul smell".

When one of the first police investigators who had been called to the building broke into the apartment, they gagged on the terrible smell coming from it.

The apartment was really hot as for some reason, the thermostat was turned way up. At the entrance was a note a neighbour had slipped under the front door, asking if the family were okay.

The TV was on and the apartment looked like it had been ransacked. Clothes were scattered across the floor, the closets had been half emptied and there were dried bloodstains all over the place.

In the bedrooms, the police found three bodies. The rotting corpse of a naked man was lying on the bed of one room while in the corner, a woman lay dead in blood-drenched clothes. On another bed, police found a second man, older than the couple, dressed in nightclothes with a pillow covering his face and a suitcase across his legs.

All three had been stabbed to death and all had been dead for over a week.

They were later identified as Lee Kui Yin, a Singaporean Chinese, her Polish husband Kazimierz Turzynski, and her father-in-law Mieczyslaw. They were all Deaf.

And that was not all.

Curled up on the floor amid all the mess, there was another shocking discovery. A small child wearing a badly soiled and filthy diaper peered silently at the police through a mound of clothes. The Turzynskis' 17-month old baby named Colleen had somehow survived for over a week in that apartment. It was her cries that neighbours had heard throughout the week she had been alone in the apartment with her murdered parents and grandfather.

She had remarkably survived by drinking toilet water (her drinking bottle with the cap still on was found in the toilet bowl) and by eating Cheerios which were scattered all over the floor.

Colleen, like her parents and grandfather, was also Deaf and of course being so little, was not able to communicate with detectives what happened in the apartment, which was so messed up not only by the killer, but by the desperate movements of the toddler to hold onto her mother and to find food that police forensic scientists found it incredibly difficult to get any sort of evidence.

Colleen was taken to hospital for dehydration and diaper rash and her godparents, another Polish immigrant couple from Connecticut, took her into their care and alerted the rest of the Turzynski family in Poland. From them, police understood that Grandfather Mieczyslaw had saved over $3000 with which he intended to go back to Poland. Police were also told that the Turzynskis were the proud possessors of a camcorder with which they recorded Colleen's daily activities to provide memories of her growing up. Both were missing from the apartment.

It was learnt that Lee Kui Yin, a seamstress, had been on holiday in the then Communist Poland when she first met and fell in love with Kazimierz, who was a mime actor in a Deaf troupe. After Kui Yin returned to Singapore, the couple wrote to each other and Kazimierz fled Poland after getting arrested for distributing anti-communist Solidarity leaflets.

Lee Kui Yin and Kazimierz Turynski before they were married in 1985.

She was 35, and he 31.

They wanted to marry and live in Singapore but Kazimierz was thwarted by visa issues, so both went to the US, and settled in New Jersey where they got married.

Kazimierz found work as a press operator at a rubber company and Kui Yin resumed her old trade as a seamstress. Their happiness was complete when Coleen was born on 13 October 1988 in Patterson, New Jersey, entitling her to US citizenship. The same year, Kazimierz' grandfather came over to find work as there was none in Poland. He lived with them in their apartment and worked variously as a carpenter, cobbler and locksmith, saving his money hard to take back to his wife and home in Poland. He kept this in a box under his bed despite the advice of friends who recommended that he put the savings in a bank. He was afraid that if he did, his status as an illegal immigrant would be discovered and he would be deported back to Poland.

In happier times, Mieczyslaw Turzynski, Baby Colleen, Kui Yin and Kazimierz Turzynski pose for a group photograph.

Investigators became aware that the Turzynskis had a Deaf friend who frequently called at their apartment, a Pakistani named Abdul Qudoos, and when they called to question him about his movements, they found a camcorder and a 35mm. camera belonging to the Turzynskis in his apartment. They also found a sum of money roughly equivalent of the amount that Mieczyslaw Turzynski was known to have saved.

Qudoos was therefore taken into custody and questioned. However, he used his deafness to avoid answering tough questions, and pretended that he did not understand the American Sign Language used in the questioning.

Qudoos insisted he was innocent and that Kazimierz had let him borrow the camcorder. Investigators felt this was unlikely as the camcorder was the Turzynskis pride and joy, with an almost complete recorded history of Colleen's upbringing still in the camera. He also could not account for his possession of nearly $3000, which comprised of Mieczyslaw Turzynski's savings.

Furthermore, he could not account for his movements around the time of the killings and was unable to provide a satisfactory and believable alibi, so he was arrested and charged with the Turzynskis' murder, as well as theft of their possessions.

Abdul Qudoos, the prime suspect in the murders.

Items and money belonging to the family were discovered in his apartment.

Qudoos was alleged to have owed the Turzynskis money. He was also alleged to be having an affair with either Kui Yin or Kazimierz. These allegations were strenuously denied.

In the meantime, Colleen's grandmother Teresa, wife of Mieczyslaw, flew in from Poland and claimed the child. Lee Kui Yin's family in Singapore also expressed an interest in bringing up the girl, as did the Polish godparents living in Connecticut. In the end, a judge ruled that Colleen would be better off with her paternal family in Poland. The deciding factor was that the paternal grandmother already had a relationship with the little girl, and all the family in Poland could use sign language.

The remains of the male Turzynskis were repatriated to Poland for burial, whilst Lee Kui Yin's ashes were sent to her family in Singapore.

The police could not pin the murders on Abdul Qudoos and after spending a year in jail, he was deported back to Pakistan and never heard of again.

The case still leaves a lot of dissatisfaction with police officials in New Jersey and the attorney's office.

"The case still haunts me," said one who was the county prosecutor at the time. "We were absolutely certain it was him, but we simply could not find the necessary evidence to convict him."

Gang Warfare along the Seafront, *De Panne, Belgium, 1991*

The Belgian seaside town of De Panne is at the westernmost point of Belgium. It sits right on the border with France and Dunkerque in France is a lot nearer to De Panne than the nearest large Belgian port of Oostende. It is an attractive and popular seaside resort with long stretches of sandy beaches and dunes.

Most of the residences on the seafront are holiday apartments to let, and in the summer of 1991, a group of Deaf Yugoslav men and women came to occupy one of the apartments on the Avenue de la Mer. The date they moved in was 21 June, and just over a week later on 1st July, they were joined by a person acknowledged as their leader, 41-year-old Mijla Illic. The 15-strong group operated a scheme, some might say a scam, along the whole of the Belgian seashore, even extending into France itself around Dunkerque.

The scam involved the selling of Deaf alphabet cards, plus trinkets or other items of minor value showing some parts of the Deaf alphabet. The band, working in threes or pairs, would distribute to diners, or other occupants of sidewalk cafés and bars, the items together with a card explaining that any monies given would be used for the benefit of Deaf people. The prime targets would be German or other foreign visitors, who would simply give them money just to be rid of their attentions.

It was quite a lucrative business, often bringing in a fair amount of money, making it worthwhile to go begging in various towns along the seafront.

The whole band were essentially homeless, and all of them dossed down in the one seafront apartment in De Panne which they rented for the summer. The whole group would use the apartment as their base, grabbing a bed if one became available but otherwise sleeping on settees or floors.

The leader, Illic, collected the money, and ensured the scheme was running smoothly and drew up an operational plan to target various towns and villages, being careful to ensure that nowhere was hit too often.

The seafront at De Panne, Belgium where the Yugoslav Deaf gang were based.

On the Thursday 11 July through to the weekend of 13/14 July, the banks in De Panne were closed due to a Flemish community holiday and festival, so four of the band travelled to Liege to exchange a considerable sum of foreign currencies for Euros to fund the band's daily living expenses.

Unfortunately, whilst in Liege, the four came across a group of seven Deaf Yugoslav men who were operating a similar scam. An argument developed in which the people from De Panne were accused of violating the territories regarded by the Liege group as theirs. Although the De Panne group denied that they were violating territories, they were followed back to De Panne by the Liege group travelling in cars. A Czech woman allied to the Liege group, together with a man from Bruges, were detailed to make themselves known to the De Penne group to find out where they were based. This information was then passed on to the leader of the Liege group.

On Thursday 11 July, the Liege group raided the apartment where the De Panne group was based and drove off those who were there with the exception of Mijla Illic who was cornered within the apartment, tortured and then stabbed repeatedly before the rival group left the apartment and fled back to Liege, taking with them all the receipts that they could find within the apartment. All the time this took place, his wife and children cowered in the apartment screaming their heads off. This sparked off a series of telephone calls to the local police station by alarmed neighbours.

There was also some evidence that the ethnicity make up of the rival groups played a large part in the killing of Illic. Around that time, Yugoslavia had descended into the Balkan war that started on 25 June and lasted until 1995. many atrocities were being committed during that War, mainly by those who were of Serbian origin.

Most of the Illic band based at De Panne were Serbians, with a few Czechs and Austrians, whereas most of the group from Liege were Croatians, bitter enemies of the Serbs.

From the outset, Belgian police found it difficult to investigate the murder of Mijla Illic, because the majority of the Deaf beggars did not speak French or understand Flemish and the sign language interpreters they had access to could not fully communicate with the Illic band because of differences in sign languages used and also the spoken languages being used.

They understood enough, however, to initiate the arrests of Petar Ljubic (aged 38) and another Croatian named Radovan Vasiljevic, aged 40, and his Czechoslovak wife, Anna Scorecova, aged 45, for participating in the murder of Mijla Illic.

Several others of the Liege group were arrested by Border police as they attempted to flee Belgium, so by the end of July, the Belgians had eight men and three women in custody for the murder of Mijla Illic. Because so many of them were Croatian, they had to import sign language interpreters from Croatia to question the arrested persons.

In the months that followed, the number of people actually charged with the murder was reduced to five individuals, with the others being released on the grounds that they understood Mijla Illic was to be given a good hiding to punish him for usurping their territory, nothing more.

On 25 October 1993, the trial of the five men began in the Assize Court of East Flanders at Bruges. Accused were Petar Ljubic, Zidic Miroslav, Kevo Bosco, Merva Radomir and Radovan Vasiljevic. It was to last for 3 weeks and the prosecution would demand the death penalty for the chief perpetrators of the crime (although in practice, in modern Belgium, the death penalty was automatically converted into life imprisonment).

The court heard that Ljubic was the leader of the Liege band of Deaf beggars, and had been the one who repeatedly stabbed his rival to death, whilst Miroslav and Bosco wielded baseball bats to batter the victim. The other two were in the apartment holding the family of Illic prisoner and ill-treating the wife.

On Monday 15 November, the jury, which had been sitting for many hours and had refused on Friday night to continue into the "wee hours of Saturday morning", finally returned the following verdicts:

- Life sentences for Petar Ljubic and Zidic Miroslav

- 20 years for Kevo Bosco

- 10 years each for Merva Radomir and Radovan Vasiljevic

The wife of the deceased, Mirjana Illic, was to receive half a million Euros damages for herself and her children.

The killer who forgot his hearing aid, *St. Louis, Missouri, USA 1998*

Joan Crotts, a 63-year-old widow, lived alone next door to a boardinghouse in St. Louis County, Missouri. The boardinghouse was used by the local authorities to house people who would otherwise be homeless, or who had just come out of prison.

In the summer of 1996, one such ex-prisoner moved into the boardinghouse. During his stay at the residence, he frequently harassed Mrs. Crotts and instigated a number of verbal confrontations with her. Typically, the incidents only involved vulgar insults by the newcomer, directed toward Mrs. Crotts. Eventually, the newcomer's behaviour intensified for the worse.

One day in August, this person and several friends assembled and began drinking in the back yard of the boardinghouse. They began throwing chicken bones to Mrs. Crotts' dogs and proceeded to toss beer cans over the fence into her yard. Mrs. Crotts, upset by the activity, came out to complain and began yelling at the group of friends, telling them to stop and quit harassing her. In response, harasser picked up a sledgehammer, smashed a rock with it, and threatened Mrs. Crotts, saying "this is your head...if you keep messing with me." There were further harsh words from group before the confrontation ended without further incident.

However, later that day, Mrs. Crotts left her house in order to attend a barbecue down the street. Apparently, she crossed through the front yard of the boardinghouse, and harasser walked down the driveway and began chastising Mrs. Crotts for walking across the lawn. He threatened her by saying, "Get your fat ass back in the house, bitch. I've got one coming for you."

At that point, Mrs. Crotts' daughter, accompanied by an acquaintance, arrived to accompany her in the walk down the street to the barbeque and saw the confrontation. Bravely, she told the harasser, who stood an intimidating six foot seven inches tall, to leave her mother alone.

Above: Mrs. Joan Crotts
and *below:* her house.
The boardinghouse can just be seen to the left.

Nothing more happened until the evening the harasser was evicted from the boardinghouse by officials accompanied by police. When Mrs. Crotts stepped out on her front porch to see what all the commotion was about, the harasser yelled at her, "I'm going to get you for this, bitch."

According to Mrs. Crotts' daughter, Debbie Decker Olive, the harasser blamed Mrs. Crotts for his eviction. He was not however moved very far - his new home was less than a mile away.

Approximately a year and a half later, in the early morning hours of March 1, 1998, Mrs. Crotts let her dogs outside. The dogs ran through an open gate in her backyard, making her suspect someone had been in the yard during the night. She investigated and found that, in addition to the open gate, a previously broken step on her back porch was out of alignment and that papers she kept in her new car were lying on the ground.

Fearing that someone had been on her property and had tampered with her car, Mrs. Crotts contacted the police. When a police officer arrived, he walked around the house and patrolled the neighbourhood in his vehicle, but found no sign of any intruder or that anything was amiss.

Mrs. Crotts remained awake, talked with her daughter on the phone and prepared to go to church. Meanwhile, the intruder (for there WAS one) who had originally opened the backyard gate, had entered Mrs. Crotts' house through an unlocked back door, went down to the basement and sat on a chair smoking cigarettes. If the police officer had been invited to search the house as well as patrol the neighbourhood, he would have found the intruder.

As it was, the intruder remained undisturbed while several hours passed. Eventually, carrying a hammer, he climbed the basement stairs and confronted Mrs. Crotts in her kitchen. He grabbed Mrs. Crotts' arm and pushed her into the living room. They sat down on the couch and began talking. Mrs. Crotts asked whether he wanted money or jewellery. The intruder said "No." He rose from the couch and forced Mrs. Crotts into an adjacent room. After collecting his thoughts, he pushed her into the rear bedroom. Once inside the bedroom, the intruder pushed her over the bed, and they lay down next to one another. The intruder exposed his penis and tried to force her to perform oral sex. However, he was unable to maintain an erection, and frustrated, hauled Mrs. Crotts and pushed her back into the kitchen. As Mrs. Crotts looked out the back door window, the intruder opened the refrigerator, and looking inside, found a two-litre Pepsi bottle. He pulled out the bottle and took a drink. He found some paper and a pen on the kitchen table and wrote "You are next" on the paper.

Then, he seized Mrs. Crotts from behind and forced her to the open door leading to the basement stairs and shoved her down the stairs, causing her to fall to the concrete basement floor. Winded and hurt, Mrs. Crotts lay face down on the concrete, unmoving as the intruder began to descend the steps, and picked up a hammer by his boot. After observing Mrs. Crotts for a time, he struck her in the back of the head several times with the hammer. He tossed the hammer toward the back of the basement and exited via the same back door through which he had entered and proceeded to Mrs. Crotts' backyard. He passed through the same gate he opened before and walked away without being seen.

In the afternoon, a neighbour who normally went to church with Mrs. Crotts, called Debra Decker Olive to report Mrs. Crotts was not answering her phone even though her car was there. This was the second call she received that day about her mother's failure to answer the phone, so she got into her car and drove over to Mrs. Crotts' home. Once there, she entered the back door leading to the kitchen and saw her mother's purse lying on the floor along with spilled Pepsi. Ms. Olive began yelling her mother's name repeatedly. From the basement, Ms. Olive heard her mother respond, "What?"

Ms. Olive went to the basement stairs and found her mother lying on the basement floor, naked except for socks and shoes and a housecoat pressed under her armpit, with a pool of blood around her head. Ms. Olive asked

Mrs. Crotts if she had been raped. Mrs. Crotts replied, "I don't know." After covering her mother and placing a towel under her head, Ms. Olive called 911 and her fiancé. An officer arrived shortly, tried to make Mrs. Crotts comfortable, and asked her what happened. Her only response was, "I don't know. I don't know."

Soon paramedics arrived, administered first aid, and eventually transported Mrs. Crotts to a hospital. That evening, while awaiting surgery, another officer spoke with her about the attack at her home. She was able to respond that a very tall and large white man, holding a hammer, had appeared at the top of the basement stairs and sexually assaulted her. She indicated that the man was very angry and after the sexual assault, he had pushed her down the basement stairs. After that, Mrs. Crotts explained that the man hit her in the back of the head with what she thought was a hammer.

Later that evening, Mrs. Crotts died in surgery of head injuries, an autopsy later finding that she had eight broken ribs and a broken hip as well as severe head injuries.

Back at the house, scene of crime officers found a hearing aid, and asked Ms. Olive if it belonged to her mother. The daughter knew her mother did not have any hearing aid, and yelled at the police, "It's him! That man who bothered my mother last year!"

Thus, with that description, the hearing aid clue and the fact Mrs. Crotts had said it had been a very tall and large white man who had also left behind his fingerprints inside the house, police had a relatively   simple task in identifying who the attacker had been. Turning up at his place of work, they took Paul T. Goodwin into custody, transporting him to St. Louis County police precinct.

Some background on Paul T. Goodwin - he had been Deaf all his life and had a low intelligence which resulted in poor grades at high school causing him to drop out despite the additional support he received in a special

Paul T. Goodwin at the time of his arrest

programme. This included communication support using American Sign Language.

He was said to have disliked attending his first school; he didn't like riding the bus to that school and he didn't like it that it had 90% Black students, and he didn't like the way they acted. He felt rejected and teased (both because of his height and his deafness) and he felt he didn't fit in. All these were given as the reason why he scored such low grades at this school.

It was also clear that he did not perceive himself as being Deaf, did not use ASL himself and refused the offer of a sign language interpreter during police questioning (which sometimes resorted to notepad and pencil!). He also waived his Miranda rights.

During questioning, he stated that he had spent the evening drinking heavily at a bar called The Bottlecap. Between 11:00 p.m. and midnight, he got a ride with a co-worker who dropped him off at a Citgo gas station. From there, Goodwin began walking and eventually arrived in Mrs. Crotts' yard, opening the gate and entering the basement as detailed above.

Arrested, arraigned and subsequently sent for trial, there has to be a question as to how much Paul T. Goodwin contributed to the eventual Guilty verdict by continuing to refuse to allow an ASL interpreter to be present and allow him to follow the trial proceedings. Indeed, there is a question as to whether Goodwin was actually able to understand what was going on. For example, the trial prosecutor injected into evidence remarks that Goodwin was racist because of his experiences at the mainly Afro-American school he went to, and that he was involved in gang-related activity. In a trial where the jury included four Black jurors, this evidence was liable to cast Goodwin in a very unfavourable light as, to most people, gang-related activity might indicate racial intolerance activities. Because he could not hear very well, even with his hearing aid, Goodwin most likely missed the opportunity of instructing his attorney to lodge an objection to that part of the evidence - perhaps as unsubstantiated or as hearsay.

This was one of his main planks in his appeal process, and it was ruled out because Goodwin failed to lodge an objection at the relevant point during his trial in 1999.

The conclusion of the trial saw Paul T. Goodwin found Guilty of Murder in the First Degree, and sentenced to death on 2nd December 1999 by lethal injection. He was then sent to Missouri's Death Row to await his execution. Over the next fifteen years, however, there was appeal after appeal, the first of which took place in April 2001, when nine points of error were raised by Goodwin and his defence team, one of which related to his alleged racist behaviour with black schoolchildren referred to above. Other points related to his mental state at the time psychological testimony was being presented about the lack of significant history of crimes of violence by Paul Goodwin. All appeals confirmed the original court ruling and death sentence.

On Monday 8 December 2014, the Supreme Court of Missouri rejected a final appeal and Missouri Governor Jay Nixon denied a clemency appeal. Two further final appeals to the US Supreme Court were also unsuccessful, and at 1:17 a.m. on 10 December 2014, the execution of Goodwin *(pictured above on 10 February 2014)* began more than an hour after it was scheduled and the 48-year-old was pronounced dead at 1:25 a.m. in Missouri's Bonne Terre State Penitentiary.

Race-hate stabbing, *Los Angeles, California, USA 2001*

Christopher and Minnie Chiu came to California from Taiwan in 1991 and settled in Laguna Hills, Orange County with their son, Kenneth. Although they tried to live with it, they could not really ignore the levels of race-hate that was directed at them, especially from their next door neighbours, the Hearns, whose son Christopher seemed to be a permanently angry young man with attitude problems towards anyone who was not white. Around the neighbourhood where he lived, he was an acknowledged white supremacist.

"He walked around the neighbourhood a lor," one of his black neighbours said. "He's a violent person and erratic. He couldn't control his impulses." She described how, one day, Christopher had raised his arm to her when she was in her frontyard and made a threatening gesture before punching her mailbox to the ground.

Living next to Christopher Hearn was like living in a tinderbox, waiting for something bad to happen. Already, the Chius had their garage door daubed in blue paint, and other instances of damage to their property. Eggs were often found splattered on their front door and windows and their car had the word "Chink" scratched into its side. Although they had never caught him in the act, they believed that Christopher Hearn was responsible for the race-hate campaign and twice police were called to the residence and Hearn questioned but no charges were brought.

On Sunday 30 July 2001, Kenneth's girlfriend from the same school that he attended, Laguna Hills High School, came over to visit and have dinner with the family. Just after 11pm, Kenneth drove her home. At that time, Christopher Hearn was seen in the garage in the next door house working on something.

Kenneth Chiu returned just after midnight and he was at a side entrance when he was attacked. Christopher Chiu said he heard screaming outside and on a hunch dialled his son's cell phone. He heard the ringing just outside the door.

Kenneth lay mortally wounded on a walkway "in so much blood," Minnie Chiu said. Her son had been stabbed at least four times. He was rushed by paramedics to the Mission Hospital Regional Medical Center where he was pronounced dead at 1:15am.

However, before he died, Kenneth Chiu told police that his assailant had been his next door neighbour, Christopher Hearn. Police officers went to his house and found him still out on his family's front porch, and placed him under arrest, at the same time recovering a knife at the scene.

Hearn, who had graduated from a programme at University High School in Irvine for students who were deaf, was held without bail at Orange County Jail for questioning with the aid of a sign language interpreter. He was then charged with the special circumstance of lying in wait and murder based on ethnicity, either of which would make him eligible for the death penalty if convicted.

Kenneth Chiu, on his 16th birthday

The defence representing Christopher Hearn chose to have a non-jury trial which opened in the Orange County Superior Court in September 2003. The main platform for the defence was an insanity plea.

The case was heard before Superior Court Judge Kazuharu Makino who, at the end of the evidence phase, found Hearn guilty of murder and special circumstance allegations of committing a hate crime and lying in wait.

Christopher Charles Hearn, aged 20.

On Thursday, September 25, it was ruled that Hearn should not go to prison, but be committed to a mental hospital. Although earlier that month, he was found guilty of first-degree murder for fatally stabbing with a kitchen knife Kenny Chiu, 17, outside their homes on July 30, 2001, he had pleaded not guilty by reason of insanity. A court-appointed psychologist testified that Hearn could not know the difference between right and wrong when he had stabbed Chiu to death.

Deputy District Attorney Carolyn Carlisle-Raines disputed that assessment, saying Hearn murdered Chiu because he disliked Asians. But Orange County Superior Court Judge Kazuharu Makino said of the killing, "In his distorted world, that's what he thought." Hearn had said he believed he was a Marine and a Ku Klux Klansman.

Makino said he was persuaded by psychiatric experts that Hearn suffered from schizophrenia and believed he had orders from the government to kill dangerous people.

Kenny Chiu's father, Christopher Chiu, 54, left the courtroom in silence visibly upset and declined to comment, but on October 13, 2003, the Chiu family announced that they would challenge the judge's ruling of insanity because they wanted the murder conviction to stand and Hearn to serve time in prison rather than in a mental health facility where he would now be sent until he is deemed no longer a threat.

Kenneth Chiu's father said the current verdict sends out the wrong message that "if you are a racist and mentally ill, it is okay to kill." He also added there was no justice for his son or his family from the judge's verdict. He also added, "We thought we could trust the American justice system."

The Pawnshop Murder, *San Diego, California, 2003*

The Gaslamp Quarter is a district of San Diego, California, covering 16½ blocks, popular with tourists and teeming with nightlife. It includes 94 historic buildings, most of which were constructed in the Victorian Era, still in use with active tenants including restaurants, shops and nightclubs.

One of these shops was the Pawn Shop on 5th Avenue owned and operated for many years by 53 year-old Gregory Angert, a native of Odessa, Ukraine.

Entrance arch to the historic Gaslamp Quarter in Downtown San Diego

At midday on Thursday 3 July 2003, the quarter was filled with tourists and downtown workers seeking lunch when someone called into the pawn shop just before 1 p.m. and discovered a body on the floor of the shop lying in a pool of blood, and called the police who were able to identify the victim as the owner of the Pawn Shop, Gregory Angert.

It was clear that he had been killed during the commission of a robbery and a nearby restaurant worker told investigating officers that he had a few minutes earlier heard two loud bangs but had dismissed this as construction noise.

Fingerprints lifted from the store's glass display cabinet were subsequently identified as coming from a Deaf man named James Shack. Police knew of him as a transit living on the streets, sometimes with his girlfriend, and it did not take them long to find him.

Actually, they found the girlfriend first and she told police officers that she had not seen her boyfriend for a little while. He had not spent the previous night with her, as was his normal routine. She also said that when she confronted him about where he had been, he had told her: "You stay out of my business. Don't ask any questions." He had then gone off without telling her where he was going.

She also said that he rented a storage unit but he would not tell her where it was and she had never been there.

It was almost a week after the killing and store robbery that James Darnell Slack was apprehended after a tip off. It seemed that he had told several other homeless people he had killed Angert, and he was still in possession of a gun, which was enough to see him arrested. This was sent for ballistics testing, which confirmed it was the gun used in the shooting.

Under questioning, he admitted shooting Angert. "I had to shoot him," he said. "He grabbed my gun. I shot him twice."

Detectives found on him a key for the storage unit, and raided it under a warrant. In the unit, they found jewellery from not only the pawnshop but also from a Chula Vista jewellery store in March 2003. In that robbery, he had pulled his gun on the owner, and got away with over $100,000 merchandise.

In a preliminary hearing in San Diego Superior Court on Tuesday 28 July,

Shack denied fatally wounding Gregory Angert, and started to say: "The victim that got shot, I know him personally," but Judge David Szumowski stopped him right there and told him to be careful as what he said in court could be used against him.

Asked if he had a lawyer, Shack said no, and said he wanted to act as his own lawyer.

Szumowski asked Shack if he could read. "I can read a little bit," Shack said, but when handed a court document outlining his legal rights, he struggled and clearly could not understand the document.

Judge Szumowski didn't like it. He said: "I think from what I have seen here today, it is an absolute total mistake that could cost you your life if you did not have a lawyer." He entered a not-guilty plea on Shack's behalf and advised that he talked to a lawyer before his next scheduled court appearance. However, before he reappeared in court, he was sent for an evaluation by a mental health expert.

In March 2004, at his next court appearance, Judge Howard Shore made a decision based on the evaluations submitted by two mental health experts to send James Shack to the Patton State Mental Hospital near San Bernardino for further evaluation on his competency to plead to the murder. In the meantime, he was sentenced to a 25 years prison term for the robbery and armed hold-up of the Chula Vista jewellery store.

When Shack finally came to trial in December 2006, more than three years after the shooting of Gregory Angert and also after countless evaluations as to Shack's mental health and competence to plead, the jury heard that the defendant entered the pawnshop just before 1 p.m. on Thursday 3 May 2003 and attempted to sell some jewellery that Angert recognised as being stolen from the Chula Vista store three months previously.

Angered, Shack pulled out his gun and attempted to rob Angert who grabbed the gun to wrestle it away but Shack shook Angert's hand off and fired the gun twice. One bullet hit the victim in the left side, piercing both lungs. Angert fell dead, and Shack ran out of the shop but not before grabbing what he could. Shack left behind a palm print and a fingerprint on Angert's glass display case.

However, the jury deadlocked 11-1 in favour of convicting Shack, prompting the judge to declare a mistrial, and ordered a status conference. The findings of this conference came up before another court session on 7 May 2007, and James Darnell Shack was declared incompetent to face a retrial, as he could not understand the charges against him and was not fit to assist in his defence.

Shack was ordered back to Patton State Mental Hospital until such a time as his mental competency is restored.

The Dad who could not cope with a disabled son, *Yorkshire, England, 2007*

Caring for a severely disabled child can put a severe strain on the parents bringing it up. Mark Meissner and Sara Hoffmann were two such parents affected by the circumstances of the birth of their child, Daniel.

Both were Deaf professionals working for a social services department in a large English city in Yorkshire, and in 2006 Sara gave birth to a baby boy. Joy turned to despair just after the birth when the parents learnt that Baby William was diagnosed with the West Syndrome, a rare and serious form of epilepsy which left him unable to sit up, hold his head up or swallow properly. Such a child might suffer up to 50 fits a day, and the baby would need 24-hour care. Baby William was also blind and deaf. You have to be strong to watch your child constantly suffer, knowing there is no hope, no cure, and having a heavy burden of needing to constantly care for it, often without much help.

Charmian Evans, the mother of a disabled son and founder of a charity called The Special Families Trust had this to say:

My son Guy was 5½ when he died in my arms, of a chest infection. On that hot June night, his tiny, twisted body finally let go of the struggle for life. He had been a near-miss cot death when he was 3½ months old, resulting in extensive brain damage. He could not sit, speak or swallow. He had fits constantly. My husband, an orthopaedic consultant, and I had to learn to titrate his drugs, pass a naso-gastric feeding tube, suction out his vomit, manually evacuate his bowels and give him stomach washouts. His cheeky smile and the glint in his beautiful eyes fed us, and the sweetness he emanated when he was not suffering would draw people to him. The light has gone from our lives since his passing fifteen years ago. My husband and I are able-bodies professionals but we found the road to support long and lonely. The fight to get anything from the authorities is exhausting. There is little help: the system has to be headbutted, often with no results.

Could I have taken my son's life? No, I could not but many times I sat by his bed and prayed, tears rolling down my face, that he might be taken and end his struggle in a life without prospects. I have a strong marriage, strong family support and many caring friends as well as the finance of being able to buy in expensive care and help. In a different place, I might not respond in the same way.

Mark Meissner was a German living in England, with family living in Germany, and therefore not able to provide any support to him in the daily struggle to care for his child. His partner Sara did have family in England but not near to where she lived, so it was difficult for them to help.

On Monday 12 February 2007, Sara Hoffman returned home from work at 5.40 p.m. to be confronted by a scene of horror. In the bathroom, she found the body of her Baby William dead in the bath with her partner comatose.

Disabled lad killed by dad

A DESPAIRING dad who drowned his disabled baby in a mercy killing was yesterday detained in

Mark Meissner had snapped, finally deciding he could take no more watching his son suffering with his severe disabilities. Mixing together a cocktail of Calpol medicine and red wine, he had fed his son then held him down in the bath until it was dead.

He then drank a full bottle of vodka and tried to drown himself in the same bath.

He left a note for his partner detailing what he intended to do, but he failed to drown himself and was still alive when found by his partner.

Paramedics who were called to the house by his distraught wife rushed both the infant and the father to hospital, where the infant was declared dead but Mark Meissner recovered and was placed under arrest.

In the Crown Court in May 2007, Gary Burrell, prosecuting, said, "This was a so-called mercy killing. It is quite clear that the defendant became significantly depressed as a result of his son's illnesses, which were demonstrably painful. He could not cope with the child's fits and was unable to watch his son's suffering."

The judge, Mr. Justice Penry-Davey, warned in his summing-up that Mark Meissner might be facing a substantial sentence: "It may be that you felt when these events occurred that you had no other course open to you than to take the life of your own son but you are in court today because nobody has the right to end the life of another human being, however desperate the situation."

He adjourned the case for the preparation of psychiatric reports.

His comments prompted Charmian Evans to say: "I have through my charity met with lots of little Williams with brave parents shackled with the crushing sentence of pain and guilt, receiving little or no support and scant financial aid. Meissner's situation was desperate. In such an impossible circumstance there is often little compassion."

She implored Mr. Justice Penry-Davey to think carefully before making any judgement.

When the case returned to court in mid-July 2007, the court was told that Meissner was devoted to his son, and one nursery worker said: "It was obvious that Mark loved William. The look of joy and love on his face when he looked at the baby spoke volumes. Tears would roll down his face if William was having a fit."

The court heard that Meissner had told the police: "I just wanted William's suffering to stop. I didn't know what else to do. I wanted him to go to sleep. I didn't want him to cry or shock. As a father I felt it was my duty to do something for my child. I couldn't watch these 20-30 fits at a time. It was awful."

Meissner pleaded guilty to manslaughter on the grounds of diminished responsibility and was ordered to be detained at a mental hospital.

His solicitor, Sally Durham, told reporters after the trial that the family believed they had been let down by the lack of support available to them.

Sara Hoffmann was reported to be sticking by the defendant. "Sara is continuing to support Mark. She'll continue to do that to try and piece their lives back together."

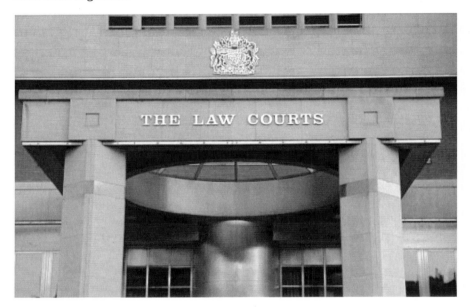

The law courts where the trial took place.

Author's Note:

Mark Meissner and Sara Hoffmann (and William) are not the real names of the people concerned. No purpose would be served in publishing their real identities.

Neighbours Feud Leads to Murder, *Frankton, New Zealand, 2010*

People living in Blackburn Street, Frankton in New Zealand's North Island had long been accustomed to the erratic behaviour of one of their neighbours, Christine Morris, aged 40. People tolerated her because she was profoundly Deaf, with a habit of writing notes to express herself, and sometimes taught some of the neighbours basic sign language. With one particular neighbour, however, there was a history of arguments which seemed to have no good reason for their origin other than Morris' belief that somehow this neighbour, Diane White, had been responsible for the local authorities taking away Ms. Morris' baby and having her committed to a mental health facility.

The trouble had started after Morris moved into an empty house next door to Diane White. The two women just did not get on, and Mrs White regularly telephoned the police and Ms. Morris' carers to complain about things her neighbour did, or was alleged to have done. This included making threats to kill her.

At the time, Christine Morris was also being treated for schizophrenia at the Henry Rongomau Bennett Centre, a mental health facility attached to Waikato Hospital.

On the morning of Tuesday 19 January 2010, police were notified by fax and telephone that Christine Morris, who was receiving treatment and staying at the Henry Rongomau Bennett Centre in Hamilton with a serious mental health illness, was missing after climbing over a fence at about 10am.

Immediately before escaping she had threatened to kill her next-door neighbour, Diane Elizabeth White, 53.

The fax sent from the Henry Bennett Centre at 10.09am was not received by Police until 11.04am, because their fax machine was out of service until just before 11am and messages were not diverted. The Henry Bennett Centre nurse followed up the fax with a telephone call to the Hamilton Police Station but received no response. She eventually called 111 at about 11.07am and spoke to the Police Northern Communications Centre (NorthComms).

At 11.13am two Police officers were dispatched to Ms Morris's address. They were unable to find her, but spoke briefly with Mrs White as she mowed her lawn, and advised her to call Police immediately if she saw Ms Morris. The officers then left.

In the meantime, Morris had called upon another neighbour who wished only to be known as Jojo but was called Ms. Y in subsequent court documents. Jojo/Ms. Y noticed that Morris was dressed strangely and in an agitated state, not realising she had fled the Henry Bennett Centre. Morris wrote on a piece of paper, as she often did: "I'm going to go and kill Diane", and was told by the other not to be silly. Jojo/Ms Y was sufficiently disturbed by Morris' behaviour to telephone the Henry Bennett Centre three times during the next hour.

Her third call prompted a response that surprised her. The nurse at the Centre said: "If you are so worried why don't you call the police yourself?"

However, the nurse at the centre was sufficiently concerned and made a second call to the police. A NorthComms dispatcher mistook the information from this call as a repeat of the information from the first call, and subsequently no officers were dispatched to Ms. Y's address to apprehend Ms Morris.

Dismayed by how events were turning out, Ms. Y watched as Morris left her house to go to another neighbour's house, emerging with a hammer that the neighbour had lent her. Ms. Y watched as Morris made her way over to Diane White's house.

Above: the victim Diane Elizabeth White

Below: the killer, Christine Judith Morris

At 12.19pm, police received a telephone call from Ms. Y reporting that Morris that just entered Mrs. White's house with a hammer. After a few minutes Ms Y telephoned again to report that Ms Morris had exited Mrs. White's house with blood on her face.

Inside her house, Ms. Y cringed as she watched Morris make her way back to her house. Screaming down the phone, she demanded immediate assistance from the police as she hid her grandchildren in the bedroom and refused to open the door while Morris banged on it loudly.

Officers were again dispatched in response to the call, to find Ms Morris. and reassure the hysterical Ms. Y. On entering Mrs. White's house, they discovered Mrs White in a pool of blood with a blood-stained hammer found nearby.

Christine Morris was arrested not long afterwards.

In July 2011, she pleaded guilty to a charge of murder in the High Court at Hamilton, and was sentenced in April 2012 to life in prison with a minimum of ten years to be served before consideration of any parole, after the court had considered psychiatric reports.

The baby that would not stop crying, *Richardson, Texas, 2013*

When police officers responded to an emergency call from a house in Shadyglen Circle, Richardson, a city in Dallas County, Texas, following a report of an unresponsive child around 5:30 a.m. on Sunday 28 April, they found that the father had the child in his arms and the baby was "pale, not breathing, and had bruises on her arms," according to a police search warrant.

The officer performed CPR until paramedics arrived and took the child to a hospital where it was discovered that the child had suffered massive trauma to back of the head, bruising to the child's back, chest, and both arms.

The baby died at the hospital. later that night at 10 p.m.

Police were called to this house at 5:30 a.m. in response to an emergency call over an unresponsive child.

In an initial police interview through a sign language interpreter who had been summoned to the house by the couple, the father who had met them at the door, Hector Rene Cupich-Quinones, 35, said that he had got up at 3:30 a.m. for a drink of water when he noticed the baby was barely breathing then had got into an argument with his wife, Maria Guadalupe Zuniga, 37 , over who was responsible for looking after the child. They had called the interpreter for assistance. It was the interpreter who had dialled 911.

The police were dissatisfied with the story and obtained an emergency search warrant to go over the house for any forensic evidence. The owner of the house where the couple were staying, Charles Niel who was also Deaf, took the police officers aside and pointed at the couple, brought his hand up to his mouth and indicated a drinking action, and invited them to look into the backyard where they found beer cans, empty whisky bottles and other containers of alcoholic beverages.

Cupich-Quinones and Zuniga were then asked to come to the police station for additional interviews, accompanied by the interpreter. At the station, Cupich-Quinones voluntarily waived his rights and agreed to answer questions. Police then called in a court-certified sign language interpreter because the original interpreter was not certified to work in criminal cases.

Through the second interpreter, Cupich-Quinones told police that he and his wife had been drinking and had gotten "into an argument over the child crying." He said he tried to give the child to Zuniga but she was "too intoxicated" and would not take the child, preferring to stay in bed trying to sleep off her drunkenness.

Cupich-Quinones admitted picking up the baby by its body and shaking it violently at around 12:30 a.m. He then told police he "hit the back of the child's head on the kitchen counter at least three times," and struck the child's face, knocking her off the counter and onto the kitchen floor.

He said the baby had been crying all night, and he was fed up with it.

He left the child with Zuniga while he went outside and smoked a cigarette. She must have put it back in the child's cot and gone back to her bed. That had been the last time he had seen the baby until he got up for his drink of water at 3:30 a.m. He had panicked when he saw that the child was so unresponsive and struggling to breathe.

Police told reporters in a press conference that Cupich-Quinones and Zuniga had got into a fight because the baby would not stop crying and Cupich-Quinones had become frustrated and started abusing the child.

"We are talking about a lot of blunt force injuries," police spokesman Sergeant Kevin Perlich said. "There was a dispute over who was going to take care of the child. It was fussy and they couldn't get her to keep quiet."

"Hector Cupich-Quinones admitted that his assaultive actions caused the death of the child and took full responsibility for committing this offense," said Perlich.

An expert paediatrician told reporters that anyone, deaf or not, would know when a child was crying. "There are tears. Babies make faces, so there are visual cues to crying aside from the sound. People who can hear would think that if you couldn't hear the crying, it would be less frustrating because what triggers is all is the sound but it was probably something about what the baby was doing that triggered the same frustration and feelings in the deaf parents."

Left: Maria Guadalupe Zuniga
Right: Hector Rene Cupich-Quinones

Both Cupich-Quinones and Zuniga were then arrested and charged with the murder of their five-month-old daughter.

After being read her rights, Zuniga invoked her right to counsel and did not provide a statement to police.

Both parents were placed in the Dallas County jail. Bail was set at $1 million for the father and $750,000 for the mother.

Author's note: As of 1 January 2015, the case had still not come up for trial.

Killers left behind mobile phone! *Mumbai, India, 2013*

Sunil and Nalini Chainani lived in a small apartment on the 10th floor of a housing society building so typical of many residences in Mumbai. They had lived in the apartment for over 30 years and during that time had watched their son and daughter grow up, and because both were deaf, had welcomed their children's friends into the apartment and enjoyed the many hours of sign language and laughter that the group of friends had brought into their lives. The fact that the group of friends all went to the same deaf school helped to cement the friendships further and many of these friends as they grew up regarded Nalini as a honorary mother.

The visits became less as the children became adults, and the couple's son moved to Australia and the daughter marrying someone from a neighbouring apartment meant the apartment became quieter. However, Nalini never stopped her welcomes if any of her children's friends happened to drop in, giving them orange juice drinks as they chatted round her kitchen table.

A typical street scene in the Pali Naka area of Bandra, Mumbai where the Chainani couple lived.

On Tuesday morning 11 June 2013, Sunil left for his employment at one of the leading electrical engineering companies in India, the Bharat Bijlee Company. Normally, during his working day, Sunil would chat with Nalini several times using the BBM facility on his Blackberry smartphone, but there was no answer from Nalini after 5:30pm.

Although a little worried, Sunil thought that maybe she had gone out or her phone battery had run down. However, when he arrived home from work around 8pm, he was concerned when the doorbell to his apartment was not answered so he used his keys to let himself into the apartment and was shocked to find his wife lying on the kitchen floor in a large pool of blood with her throat slit.

With the help of his neighbours, Sunil got her to Lilavati Hospital where she was declared dead on arrival. Doctors there reported the suspicious death to police who took Sunil back to the apartment, once it transpired that was where the killing had happened.

Police investigators were not especially pleased to find that the crime scene was so badly compromised, not just because the body had been removed but because countless neighbours had also accessed the apartment to help to carry Nalini down to ground level to take her to hospital. Some of them had in fact walked into the pool of blood and left bloody footprints everywhere.

Still, forensic experts did the best they could in the circumstances. Some of the clues they found in the apartment included the fact that there were no apparent signs of forced entry. They also found two glasses on a tray with remains of water, indicating that the victim knew her killers. Nalini was also in the process of making orange juice for them.

Police also found three mobile phones in the kitchen, one of which Sunil said did not belong to the family. This phone gave off repeated text alerts, indicating that there were several incoming text messages to the phone. Investigators were ordered to trace the source of these text messages to

A police spokesman announcing on India's TV9 channel the murder of Nalini Chainani (pictured on the right of the screen).

determine where they were coming from.

In the meantime, police enquiries elicited from local questioning that two men had been seen outside the building for most of Tuesday. Their frequent and obvious use of sign language drew attention to them. A number of other residents were used to seeing sign language being used in the building and the locality because of the couple's deaf children and the presence of their friends.

Some of the residents said they recognised one of the men as a regular visitor to the apartment when the couple's son had been living there prior to his moving to Australia. They said that this man had lived in a neighbouring apartment block which was now undergoing refurbishment, necessitating temporary relocation of its residents.

Questioning a security guard, they learnt that he had logged the two men into the building at 4pm and logged them exiting just after 7pm, which corresponded with the estimated time of the murder.

This identification, plus the police accessing the mobile phone text messages meant that they were able to apprehend the main suspects within 24 hours, of the murder, despite the compromised crime scene.

The first to be arrested was Parvez Wahid Khan, the 30-year-old son of a local doctor. He had been a trainer in a local gym, but was now unemployed. He was held because police had traced the owner of the mobile phone who said he had lent it for the day to Khan who, because of his unemployment, could not now afford a phone.

Parvez Khan refused to say anything, even when his father was brought in to assist the police in interpreting for them. Police learnt, however, the name of his accomplice, Saif Hussain Bhavnagri, a coffee shop worker who was soon also in custody after a struggle where the public assisted police.

India's TV9 channel announcing the arrest of the two suspects.

28-year -old Saif Hussain was a childhood friend of the Chainani's son and daughter. Together with his Deaf sister, Saif Hussain had gone to school with them and had spent many hours in the Chainani apartment being welcomed by Nalini Chainani. Their visits had become less frequent as they had grown up, but because Saif Hussain lived in the next apartment block where his family owned a one-room kitchen apartment, he was still a frequent visitor, even after the Chainani's son had moved to Australia and the daughter had married into a family living in the next apartment block where Saif Hussain also lived.

Police found that Saif Hussain had in fact visited the Chainani apartment frequently in the previous month. He denied that he was having a sexual relationship with Nalini Chainani, who at age 58, was 30 years older than he was, but admitted to police that he and Parvez Khan had been plotting to rob the apartment for several months, having noticed that there was money and jewellery often lying around. However, both recognised that they would not be able to escape being identified by Nalini Chainani, so they would have to kill her. They were afraid, however, of taking that step further.

The two Deaf murderers, wearing hoods, being paraded by police before being taken to court.

It was discovered that the suspects had stolen over Rs. 6 lakhs (approximately 6300 British pounds or 9700 US dollars), plus a quantity of expensive jewellery, all of which police recovered before they could be disposed of, such was the speed of their arrests.

The murder of Nalini Chainani shocked her neighbourhood and the some of the Mumbai deaf community who remembered their welcoming kindness whenever they visited their apartment.

Saif Hussain Bhavnagri and Parvez Wahid Khan were charged under the Indian Penal Code sections 302 for murder, 392 for robbery and 397 for robbery with attempt to cause grievous hurt or death, and remanded in custody to await trial.

As of January 2015, this trial has still not taken place.

The Jealous Killer, *Leicester, England, 2014*

When Jill Brown*, a 43-year-old Deaf woman, decided to discontinue her relationship with a Deaf man some 15 years her junior and took up with another Deaf partner some 15 years older than she was, she little realised she had set in motion a terrible sequence of events.

In actuality, Jill had been seeing both men for some time, flitting between them, before deciding to live with her older lover, 58-year-old Christopher Penman, a divorcee, at his house in Beaumont Leys, Leicester.

This enraged the younger man, an Iraqi refugee named Awat Akram, who began to stalk the couple and make threats against them. Jill Brown and Christopher Penman became so frightened that they sought refuge in a safe house in Loughborough. In two weeks from 10 February 2014, the pair stayed in two separate safe houses, but on the morning of Friday 21 February, Penman was told he could not stay in the safe house, so he returned home, leaving Brown there.

Awat Akram

Akram was born deaf in Iraq and received no education. Growing up in a low level existence, he made a living cleaning shoes. After watching his family suffer during the turmoil that was Iraq after the first Iraqi War during which he had his nose broken by an American soldier's rifle butt, he escaped the country and eventually arrived in Leicester where he was befriended by Christopher Penman who introduced him to the Leicester deaf community.

Through his association with Penman, he met Jill Brown and the three of them began associating together, going to pubs and deaf community events.

During 2013, Akram took Brown to a religious ceremony at a mosque and told her afterwards - to her astonishment as she had not understood the significance of the occasion - that they were now man and wife. Jill Brown rubbished the statement and continued to see Christopher Penman.

During Christmas 2013, Akram, Penman and Brown were together at a bingo event when Akram was seen making explicit threats in sign language at Penman and Brown indicating he would kill one or both of them. Both Penman and Brown left the event and went home, but continued to be stalked and receive text messages from Akram demanding the return of "his wife", which eventually led to their seeking refuge in Loughborough.

When Penman returned to his house in Somerfield Walk, Beaumont Lays, he was in a fearful state, and thought that he spotted Akram loitering outside the house.

Across the road from where Penman lived was another Deaf house occupied by a Christian Fellowship pastor named Robert McFarland and his wife Gabriele, who were shocked to receive a visit from Penman late on Friday evening, 21 February. McFarland said that Penman was "looking scared". A few minutes later, a text message was received by Penman. It was from Akram demanding that he "open" the door.

Looking out of their window, the McFarlands spotted Akram "walking back and forth" near Penman's home, and decided to call the police but by the time they arrived at about 10:30pm, Akram had gone, and the officers found no trace of him when they searched the neighbourhood.

After some discussion with the three police officers, Penman decided to go home and the police officers escorted him there at about 12:40am.

Later Mr. McFarland was to sign in court: "I watched him go. I was relieved to see he was with them, and I remember watching him go inside the house." He added that was the last time he saw his good friend alive.

The next afternoon, Penman's friends tried unsuccessfully to contact him. When they spotted signs of a break-in at Penman's house, they decided to call the police. Christopher Penman was found dead under a bloody duvet - his bed was saturated with blood and he had received multiple stab wounds.

There was only one suspect - Awat Akram. He was soon arrested at his home in another part of Leicester.

Christopher Penman

In Leicester Crown Court in September 2014, Awat Akram stood trial for the murder of Christopher Penman and was sentenced to 28 years in jail, which brought thunderous clapping from the family and friends of Penman in the courtroom.

Earlier, Judge Michael Pert had told Akram in court: "This was a planned, savage and merciless execution. In killing Mr. Penman, you deprived society of a decent, affable and good hearted man. You deprived his family of a devoted brother, father and grandfather. You did it because you are a jealous, selfish, manipulative and dangerous young man. After breaking into Mr. Penman's house at about 3am, you stabbed him 23 times as he slept in his bed, then went home and watched computer porn."

A statement read on behalf of Penman's family read: "We have lost a very inspirational father-in-law, uncle, brother and very special granddad to our children. Dad was a good person; he would not have hurt a soul. Everyone in the deaf community will also miss him."

Author's Note:

*Jill Brown is not the real name of the person concerned. No purpose would be served in publishing her real identity.

Book II

Introduction

As this is likely to be the last book that I shall write about Deaf murders, I thought I would include a number of cases that have been on my "shelf" for a number of years waiting for an opportunity to be published.

These cases are about Deaf people who have been **murdered**.

Several of these cases are unusual and deserve to be read by all those with an interest in Deaf crime. All the murderers are either "hearing" persons (i.e non-Deaf) or are unsolved.

The Serial Killer, *Alabama, USA 1986*

The Alabama Institute for the Deaf and the Blind covers a sprawling site in Talladega comprising of a variety of residential dormitories and apartment buildings sited around the campus that includes the Alabama School for the Deaf, the Alabama School for the Blind, the Helen Keeler School, the EH Gentry Center, a full service education and rehabilitation facility for the adult Deaf, Deaf-blind and Blind, and various vocational training sites grouped under the Alabama Industries for the Blind. The whole Institute provides education for a whole range of ages from the very young to those who are adults.

On 24 February 1986, a counsellor responsible for the education and development of a mature Deaf student became concerned after learning that she had missed a week of classes without explanation. It was also learnt that the student's sons aged four and five had also not attended their kindergarten classes, neither had she been answering her TTY (a device that functions as a telephone for Deaf people).

The manager of the dormitory block, where the student had an apartment, was telephoned and asked to check on her welfare. After receiving no answer to the ringing of the apartment bell, the manager used her pass key to let herself in, and found 24-year-old Sherri Weathers dead in her room, along with her two sons, Chad and Joseph.

The bodies were piled together on Sherri's bed and loosely covered with a blanket. The manager called the campus security police who in turn called homicide investigators.

Whilst waiting for them to arrive, the manager realised that another student had been missing from the Institute for some time and when the police arrived, they were directed to another apartment, occupied by a 33-year-old Deaf woman named Linda Jarman. Inside, patrolmen found her naked and decomposed body on the bed, a television set and the woman's car apparently stolen by her assailant. All four victims had been strangled.

Above: The main building at Alabama Institute for the Deaf and Blind

Below: The main entrance to the campus, with the year it was founded, 1858.

The bodies were too badly decomposed to say whether the victims had sex before their deaths. An urgent roll-call and investigation was held at the school to find out if there were any more victims who might not have been seen for at least a week.

Police investigators learnt that an Institute art teacher, one "Daniel Spence," had expressed a romantic interest in Sherri Weathers. This interest had not been reciprocated by Ms. Weathers. It was further learnt that "Spence" had not been seen since February 20. It was found that "Spence" had turned up at the school several months earlier, offering to teach art for free in hopes of gaining a permanent job later on. He was indeed a talented artist.

Fingerprints extracted from the murder scenes at the school identified "Spence" as Daniel Lee Siebert, convicted of the Las Vegas manslaughter of a man in 1979 who died of 29 stab wounds. For this he was sentenced to ten years in prison but escaped in 1981. While he was at large, he abducted

A fuzzy photograph of Daniel Lee Siebert, taken at the time he was at the school in Alabama

a woman in her car but she escaped whilst travelling at 55 mph over a San Francisco bridge. For this, he got another ten years in prison but was paroled in September 1985. He jumped the $25,000 bond and arrived in Talladega in January 1986. With other evidence, police were also able to link Siebert with the strangulation of a 19 year old black prostitute in Calhoun County, a few miles north of Talladega. This victim, Sheryl Evans, was found the day after the other killings dumped by the side of a road. She was last seen alive a week earlier.

Detectives also learned that Siebert had been dating Linda Odum, a 32-year-old cocktail waitress from Talladega who was reported missing on February 24. At first, it was thought that she was assisting Siebert in his escape, especially as her car was also missing - Jarman's car left in its place.

However, Highway patrol officers found Linda Odum's car abandoned near Elizabethtown, Kentucky, on March 3, 1986, and Siebert's fingerprints were lifted from the vehicle. Police then began to fear that Linda was another victim, a fear that was confirmed when her naked, decomposed remains were found outside of Talladega on March 30. She had also been strangled.

Over the next six months, sightings of the fugitive were reported from Ohio, New Jersey, Nevada, Southern California, and Montreal, Canada. The first solid lead came on September 3, when a Las Vegas friend of Siebert's reported a telephone call from the fugitive.

Police were ready when the next call came, and it was traced to a pay phone in Nashville, Tennessee. Employees at a nearby restaurant identified Siebert's mug shots, and he was arrested next morning, when he arrived to complete some work on the restaurant's sign.

In custody, Siebert readily confessed to the five murders in Alabama. He also confessed to various others spanning the United States and Canada. How many? "Maybe a dozen," he said. "Maybe more. I try to put those things out of my mind." He killed for purposes of sex and robbery, being careful to murder his victims after a San Francisco hooker survived a throttling and filed charges against him.

Through tracing his fingerprints and other forensic evidence, police were able to link him to, and charge him with, the murders of two black prostitutes in California named Gidget Castro, aged 28, and Nesia McElrath, aged 23. McElrath's body was found on December 19, 1985, in a rural area near Castaic, a community about 40 miles north-west of Los Angeles and Castro's body was found a week later in an alley near the 4600 block of East Washington Boulevard in the City of Commerce, also in Los Angeles.

At first, these killings had been attributed to the so-called Southside Slayer who was leaving victims all over the south side of Los Angeles. Like most of the Southside victims, both women were black, both were prostitutes and both had been strangled, but following Siebert's confession, and due to forensic evidence, it was accepted that these two women were killed by Daniel Lee Siebert.

Police also found that while on the run from the Alabama killings, Siebert had surfaced in New Jersey where he joined a day-outing organised by a tourist company to Caesar's Casino in Atlantic City, New Jersey. Somehow, Siebert found himself alone in a hospitality suite with the tour guide, 57-year-old Beatrice McDougall. He then stabbed and strangled her for no other reason than just to get the money she was carrying.

Mass Killing Suspect Charged
In Mrs. McDougall's Murder

By JEFF WILKIN
Gazette Reporter
With Wire Reports
A 22-year-old drifter and artist, a resident of Alabama's death row linked to at least 10 killings, yesterday was charged with the murder of Beatrice McDougall of Rotterdam.

Danny Lee Siebert was charged with

when the man has told me he has people," said his attorney, George Sims said Siebert expressed no over the slayings of the three wo Talladega, "but did indicate some c over killing the two small children Siebert told investigators he kill children because he did not want

Newspaper Headline relating to the McDougall murder and *(left inset)* the victim

Mrs. McDougall's murder was the first murder ever to happen inside an Atlantic City casino since casinos started operating in 1978.

In April 1987, Daniel Lee Siebert was sentenced to death for the murder of Linda Jarman at the Alabama Institute for the Deaf and Blind - the first time that anyone had ever been sentenced to death for a murder in a deaf school. Four months later, Siebert was given another death sentence for the other murders committed in the school. All other cases were kept on file.

The full number of victims for which Danny Lee Siebert was tried (or had placed on file) were:

- Sherri Weathers, 24
- Chad Weathers, 5
- Joseph Weathers, 4
- Sheryl Evans, 19
- Linda Odom, 32
- Linda Jarman, 33
- Gidget Castro, 28
- Nesia McElrath, 23
- Beatrice McDougall, 57
- unnamed victim
- unnamed woman

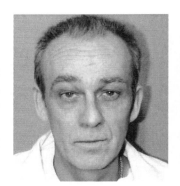

Siebert spent 21 years fighting his death sentence through various appeals courts but finally, all appeals exhausted, Seibert's execution date was set for October 25, 2007 for the murders of Weathers and her children. However, Siebert had been undergoing treatment for pancreatic cancer so his execution was delayed hours before it was to occur.

Seibert died Tuesday, April 22, 2008, apparently of complications from cancer, so in the end, although he died, he had cheated legal execution.

Daniel Lee Siebert, just weeks before his death from pancreatic cancer

Did he? Or didn't he? *Knoxville, Tennessee, USA 1998*

Jennifer Byerley was known, in American parlance, as a bar-fly - someone who frequented bars and consorted with men who also frequented these bars. Deaf from birth, she could only communicate in sign language, or with those who did not understand sign language, through written notes and habitually carried a small notepad and pen for this purpose.

One of the bars that she regularly frequented was the End Zone bar[1] on Alcoa Highway near the Knoxville Airport. This was within walking distance from her apartment, and she was a regular at the End Zone bar, known to the bar staff and in particular one waitress who also had an apartment in the same complex that Jennifer Byerley lived in. Byerley was 22 years-old and unemployed, living on Social Security payments.

On the night of 11 March 1998, Byerley was in the bar as usual, and communicating with a group of Mexicans who also frequented the bar. The communicating was done by means of gestures and also by writing. The Mexicans were friends of Byerley's former boyfriend, Marco Villa-Gomez, who was currently on charges of domestic assault on Byerley with the trial scheduled to happen on 8 April 1998.

It seemed to the staff of the End Zone bar that the Mexicans were hassling and haranguing Byerley, causing her visible distress and one of them, Mary Roberts who was also Byerley's neighbour, went over to the group and asked the Mexicans to leave. The victim, who was crying, stayed in a booth. When she returned to the bar counter, one of the other customers whom Ms. Roberts had seen in the bar several times previously, asked about the woman and then obtained paper and pencil (so that he could communicate with the deaf woman) before going to sit with her in the booth. Ms. Roberts saw the two pass notes before the other man stood up, wadded the paper, threw it in a trash can, and remarked to the room in general, "How in the hell did I get myself into this shit?" The man then went to the restroom then

[1] This bar no longer exists.

exited through a back door at about 11:30 p.m. Byerley left later through the front door, still visibly upset. Another staff member of the End Zone, a bartender named Earl Horton who knew Jennifer Byerley and the other person, who he named as Douglas Jordan, as patrons of the bar, followed Byerley outside and asked in basic sign language with the thumbs up sign whether she was "okay."

Because he was concerned for her safety, he walked to the edge of the building to watch her progress and saw that Jordan was standing outside the building and Byerley walked up to him. Horton asked if they were "okay."

Jordan replied, "Yes, we're fine." Byerley turned round to look at Horton and nodded her head affirmatively. Horton watched the two walk away in the direction of the motel next door.

At approximately 6:30 a.m. on Thursday March 12, the body of Jennifer Byerley was discovered in a curve along the side of Wheeler Road in Blount County about 1.2 miles from the End Zone bar and less than ½ mile from her apartment. The victim was on her back. One leg was crooked and one arm of her jacket was pulled over her head and face. Her throat was cut. There was blood on the jacket and frost on the sleeve. She was wearing three rings. She wasn't formally identified until the following Monday March 16.

In the meantime, when Mary Roberts saw Jordan again the day after the incident in the bar and before Byerley's body had been identified, she noticed scratch marks down the side of his face she could not remember seeing the night before. They were still there when Horton saw him the day afterwards. On both occasions, Jordan explained that he had a skin condition and had scratched himself.

Once they had identified Byerley, police investigators led by Blount County Sheriff's Department Detective Scott Carpenter, conducted a search of Byerley's apartment where there were no signs of a struggle, then questioned staff at the End Zone Bar who told Carpenter that Byerley had been seen in the company of both a group of Mexicans who had been bothering her, and a white male named Douglas Jordan.

Police also had a report from Byerley's next door apartment neighbour stating that there had been a disturbance around 3:00 a.m. coming from Byerley's apartment. This had woken him up, and he had heard a voice shouting angrily in Spanish which he did not understand, followed by a small number of grunts, which he said was just about the only noise that Jennifer Byerley could make. This did not surprise him because Byerley frequently hung around with Mexicans and often spent her Social Security disability money on them. He said he knew Byerley fairly well because she would sometimes knock on his door and hand over notes begging for money.

This report was not acted upon by police because by then they had searched Douglas Jordan's room at the Airport Inn and discovered blood in his bathroom sink and a crumbled note found in the garbage can underneath the sink. There was also blood found on his sheets.

Interviewed five days later on March 17, Jordan acknowledged that he was angry with Byerley on the night of the murder because they "had to have the same conversation again" and "she couldn't take no for an answer." He denied, however, that he had been angry enough to kill her and further denied having hit her or harmed her in any way. He also denied having sex with Byerley. When asked about the blood on his sheets, the defendant explained that he had a skin condition that caused him to become injured and bleed easily. When questioned about blood that was found around his bathroom sink, Jordan told the officer that he had been injured in a car accident five days earlier. He agreed to provide police with blood and hair samples and consented to have his car impounded for examination. When asked to account for his time since the murder, the defendant reported to the officer that he had performed a variety of personal errands, which in-cluded taking his laundry to The Laundry Place on Chapman Highway. This was confirmed by the laundry manageress who said that Jordan had paid extra to have the bed sheets, which had large amounts of blood, done the same day. This had been on March 12. She said that she had needed to use bleach to try and get rid of the bloodstains, but had not been entirely successful as some remained.

The note, which Jordan helped the officer read, was deciphered as follows:

Byerley: *I'm so sorry. I not mean. I'm so drunk.*

Jordan: *You make me look like a fool and me want nothing to do with you. I want you to go home. I told you I did not want you for girlfriend and that's what I meant. I just want to be free and have fun, period. If there were any chance of us you just ruined it. Do you want me to take you home?*

Byerley: *Can I stay with you tonight? Did you stop by my house . . . after your work?*

Jordan: *No! I did not stop by your house.*

Byerley: *Do you want me to go home?*

Jordan: *Yes and no. I don't want you to be close to me!!!!!!! I do not want you as girlfriend. Just for fun! Do you want to go home or do you want to stay here and fuck?*

After initially denying that Byerley had not been in his room at the Airport Inn, Jordan admitted that Byerley had been in the room for *"...maybe 15-20 minutes..."*, roughly the length of time it had taken to hold the written conversation. Jordan said that after the written conversation and not wishing to *"fuck"* as he put it, Byerley had left his room and he had not seen her since. Although he had offered, again, to drive her home, she had declined and staggered off, really drunk.

When arrested for the murder, Jordan allegedly told Detective Carpenter that he never had any physical contact with the victim, even when another police officer falsely told him that Byerley's blood had been identified on his sheets. Jordan had always been confident that police would not find any forensic evidence that would link him to the killing, simply because he had not killed or harmed the girl. He insisted that any forensic evidence were errors, stating that *"Something isn't right.. there's got to be something somewhere somebody ain't seeing."*

Douglas Franklin Jordan, Jr. finally came up for trial on 15 October 2002, over 4½ years after the murder, before Judge D. Kelly Thomas at the Blount County Courthouse. Much of the delay had been due to the obstinate refusal of Jordan to admit to killing Byerley, and continuing to insist that he was innocent.

There were also legal arguments over the admissibility of medical and other evidence that could be presented at the trial.

The Blount County Courthouse in Maryville, Tennessee where Douglas F. Jordan stood trial for the killing of Jennifer Byerley, a killing which he denied.

The court heard from Detective Scott Carpenter that Jordan had admitted lying in an interview following Byerley's death, to which the defence responded that Jordan had been nervous and had made a mistake, which he subsequently corrected. Carpenter acknowledged, however, that Jordan had always co-operated fully with the police investigation, insisting that because he was not interested in a relationship with Byerley and only wanted sex with her, she had left his residence after fifteen minutes.

The court also heard from Mary Roberts and Earl Horton that Jordan had been seen leaving the vicinity of the End Zone Bar with Byerley, and that as far as the police knew, this had been the last time Byerley had been seen alive.

Dr. David M. Gilliam, who performed the autopsy, estimated that the victim had been dead for three to five hours when the body was found. He testified that although the victim's throat had been cut, the cause of death was manual strangulation. The victim also had blunt force injuries to the head and face and a non-lethal stab wound to the upper right abdomen, which Dr. Gilliam believed, based on bleeding and bruising patterns, to have occurred prior to death. Dr. Gilliam characterized the victim's neck wound as "gaping" and described it as "consistent with someone being on top of, kneeling over, or sitting on top of the victim and cutting from the victim's right to left." It was his opinion that a right-handed person inflicted the neck injuries.   Douglas Jordan was right-handed.

Three witnesses, including Jordan's stepfather, testified that on March 8, Jordan had been in an automobile accident and had wrecked his car. The stepfather, Mike Michaels, testified that the defendant telephoned him at approximately 4:30 a.m. on March 8 to request assistance after an automobile accident. He recalled that he picked the defendant up at his residence at the Airport Inn and drove to the scene of the accident on Maloney Road. According to Michaels, the defendant had lost control of his vehicle, gone over a twelve-foot embankment, and struck a tree. Michaels recalled that the defendant had a number of cuts and bruises, including some on the face. He testified that he and Jordan's mother helped clean and dress the wounds, remembering that they "pulled glass out of Jordan's head for about an hour."

Jordan's defence attorney contended that this accounted for Jordan's obvious scratches after the murder and the reason why blood was found in his bathroom sink. He pointed out that none of the victim's blood had been found inside Jordan's room.

Defence Attorney Jeffrey Whitt (for Jordan) emphasised the testimony of Byerley's neighbour David Cockrill, who had described overhearing a male voice shouting angrily in Spanish, which he could understand and contended that the police investigators had not given sufficient weight to this report as this would prove Jennifer Byerley was still alive at least two-three hours after she was alleged to have been in Jordan's hotel room.

There were six key stipulations of fact relating to the medical and forensic evidence presented in the case:

1. Jordan's blood was on the side of his motor vehicle and also was found on the console inside of the same vehicle; no other person's blood was found in or on the vehicle.

2. Jordan's and Byerley's blood were found mixed on the right front of the Byerley's black corduroy overalls and on the rear tag on the inside of the her bra.

3. Jordan's blood was found on the sheets seized by officers at his residence. None of Byerley's blood was found on the bed sheets.

4. Jordan's blood was found on the note seized by officers at his residence. None of the victim's blood was found on the note.

5. Jordan's DNA was found under the index and ring finger nail scrapings of the victim's right hand.

6. Byerley's blood was found only on her person and the clothes she was wearing.

Defence Attorney Whitt told the court that Jordan could not explain how his DNA came to be on the overalls and the bra, but guessed this could have happened through contact at the Airport Inn before they arrived at his residence, because Byerley never removed her clothes whilst there, and did not stay more than 15 minutes. There was a possibility that contact could have been made when Jordan refused Byerley's advances and told her to go home.

The jury chose not to believe Douglas Jordan and found him guilty of second degree murder.

During the sentencing phase, Assistant District Attorney James Brooks recommended that Jordan receive a maximum sentence of 25 years, citing as an enhancing factor the brutal, senseless and exceptionally cruel way Jennifer Byerley had died. He said that she had been beaten and stabbed before she was strangled and had been fully aware of her impending death. He also stated that Jordan's prior criminal behaviour was a key factor in his recommendation for the maximum amount of time allowed by law.

Brooks called a witness, a young woman who had been Jordan's girlfriend for a time. She testified that he had hit her in the face and slammed her car door on her one evening after he had apparently used a drug of some kind.

However, Jordan's attorney said that he found it very difficult to argue for the sentencing a man who had not committed a crime. He asked the court to note that Douglas Jordan had consistently denied harming or killing Jennifer Byerley, proclaiming his innocence and had given full co-operation in the investigation of Byerley's death, so this should be a migrating factor in regard to the length of his sentence.

"He had," Whitt said, "opened up his entire life to cooperate in an effort to clear himself, firmly pinning his faith in the American justice system."

Circuit County Judge D. Kelly Thomas said he had reviewed a pre-sentence report on Jordan as well as victim impact statements provided by Byerley's mother and aunt prior to hearing arguments.

He stated that the two enhancing factors cited by Attorney Brooks - prior criminal history and use of deadly force - had led him to impose the maximum of 25 years, but the migrating factor cited by Whitt had prompted a two-year reduction, so Jordan was sentenced to 23 years in prison. Judge Thomas imposed an order that Jordan had to serve 85% of his sentence before being considered for parole. This meant it would be 2021 before Jordan could apply for parole.

However, Douglas Jordan continued to protest his innocence but failed in his appeals in 2005 and 2009 before a third appeal in 2011 agreed that the prosecution had withheld two important facts from the defence that might have helped his case at trial, and overturned the original conviction, ordering that a re-trial be held.

Douglas F. Jordan, at the hearing that overturned his original conviction.

Author's Note:

Douglas Franklin Jordan had NEVER admitted his guilt, and has always insisted that the forensic evidence that convicted him was flawed. Because of this, has always protested his innocence.

His chance will come at his re-trial which is scheduled for 24 March 2015.

Knock on car window leads to murder, *Singapore, 2001*

Krishnan Sengal Rajah had just finished his shift with Diethlem Industries, Singapore, a distributor for foods & confectionery, health & personal care, stationery & office supplies, especially nuts, canned provisions, snack food, and toiletries to the aircraft industry at Changi Airport and had just ordered a gift for his daughter's forthcoming 16th birthday when he bumped into a Deaf friend, Chandrasegaran Raman in Dunlop Street, Little India, an Indian quarter in Singapore. Together, the two Deaf friends decided to go for a drink at Rajini Wine Bar, where one drink morphed into four quarter-litre bottles of gin.

Dunlop Street in Little India, Singapore
where Krishnan went shopping for his daughter's 16th present
and bumped into a Deaf friend, before going to a nearby bar for drinks.

At Chandrasegaran's suggestion, the two friends then went to the nearby Back Alley Pub at 10:30 pm for another drink before calling it a night on 30 June 2001 and deciding to go home. Emerging from the pub, they walked back down Dunlop Street, where they would part and go their different ways.

The Back Alley Pub in Singapore on the right where the
two Deaf friends had their last drink.

As the Deaf pair walked down the street, a 28-year-old Chinese crane driver, Tan Chun Seng, was parking his newly purchased Nissan Sunny car along a street. Just as he was parking the car, he saw the two Indian males walking towards his car. They were Krishnan and Chandrasegaran. Tan had never met these two men before. Just as they approached the car, Chandrasegaran, who was not holding his drink very well, overbalanced and hit the glass window on the front passenger side of the car. Tan was furious that this had happened to his new car.

Krishnan and Chandrasegaran stopped at the rear of the car. The latter was gesturing to Tan in his car, with Krishnan standing beside him. All this happened when Tan was in the midst of parking his car. He was set on confronting Chandrasegaran, but by the time he had parked and got out, the two Indians had moved away.

Tan walked a short distance to catch up with the two men but soon realised that Chandrasegaran was no longer in sight, having gone his separate way from Krishnan. Not being able to confront Chandrasegaran about why he hit his car, Tan decided to approach Krishnan. Trying to catch up with Krishnan, Tan was shouting at him, asking him why his friend had hit his car. The fact that Krishnan continued walking, unperturbed at Tan's outburst, further enraged Tan. Tan was unaware that Krishnan was a deaf mute. He started to hurl Hokkien vulgarities at Krishnan. When Tan had almost caught up with Krishnan, the latter sensed - perhaps from the reactions of the people around him - that something was happening behind him and turned around and came face-to-face Tan.

Krishnan, now facing Tan, just stood his ground and looked at Tan, slightly puzzled. Tan kept on hurling Hokkien vulgarities at Krishnan. Tan coupled his verbal outburst with expressive hand gestures. Krishnan, however, being a deaf mute, did not say anything in reply. Tan noticed that Krishnan was of a big physical build. As Tan continued his verbal onslaught and hand gesturing, he moved forward thereby closing the gap between himself and Krishnan. Krishnan, perhaps feeling threatened, then pushed Tan with great force such that Tan immediately fell backwards and landed on his backside on the ground. This push was not an ordinary shove. It was meant to fell Tan to the ground.

After being pushed to the ground, Tan spotted a wooden pole on top of a pile of rubbish at the side of the street. Convinced that he was not going to overpower Krishnan in a bare-hand fight, Tan grabbed the pole, got up, and gave chase to Krishnan who had walked on a few steps from the place where he had pushed Tan. Witnesses were later to say that Tan hit Krishnan numerous times with the pole but only one really connected with the head.

Krishnan then fell to the ground and lay motionless. Most of Tan's hits with the wooden pole appeared to have hit Krishnan on the back where he was wearing a haversack. Tan threw the wooden pole to the side of the road, walked back to his car and drove off. Several bystanders who had witnessed the incident called police and an ambulance. The paramedic who arrived pronounced Krishnan dead.

Later, an autopsy report would confirm that the death had stemmed from a constellation of injuries over the right side and the right back of the head consistent with being hit with severe blow over the right side of the head.

Tan Chun Seng was traced to his family residence on Johor Baru, on the Malaysian side of the Singapore Straits where he was arrested by the Malaysian police on an extradition warrant executed by the Singapore police. Tan had opposed extradition proceedings but his opposition was over-ruled by the Malaysian courts.

When Tan came up for trial in February 2003, the High Court learnt of the fracas that had developed out of a simple bump to Tan Chun Seng's new car and how Tan had been so enraged at the perceived ignorance of his shouts at Krishnan's back, not realising that Krishnan was Deaf.

Languages were in fact a feature of the trial. Tan only spoke Hokkien, a form of Malaysian Chinese dialect found predominately in Johor Baru and the island of Penang. He needed a Hokkien-speaking interpreter in court. On the other hand, Krishnan had been Deaf and conversed mainly in Singaporean Sign Language, which he had learnt in the deaf school in Singapore. Krishnan's widow, Neelachi Singaram, and his friend Chandrasegaran Raman were of the same age and had also gone to the same school, and sign language was needed in court to translate Chandrasegaran's testimony and to keep Krishnan's Deaf family and friends informed of the proceedings.

Tan's defence was that he had been provoked by Krishnan's shove. This was not accepted by Justice Choo Han Teck who said that a shove, or push, no matter how violent or unrestrained, could not justify the beating leading to murder that was inflicted on Krishnan.

Tan Chun Seng was totally shocked to be sentenced to death by the court, and immediately appealed.

The appeal came up before the Singapore Court of Appeal in June 2003.

The old Supreme Court Building in Singapore.
All courts were relocated to a brand new building in 2006

At the appeal, there were legal arguments over the differences between 'sudden fight' and premeditated murder. The three Appeal Court judges ruled that *"culpable homicide is not murder if it is committed without premeditation in a sudden fight in the heat of passion upon a sudden quarrel, and without the offender having taken undue advantage or acted in an   unusual manner. "*

The judges stated that although Tan had admitted hitting Krishnan *'numerous times'* and this had been confirmed by eye-witnesses, medical evidence was clear that only one blow by the pole wielded by Tan had actually landed on Krishnan's head and was the cause of death; all other blows seemed to have landed on the haversack on Krishnan's back.

It was ruled that the death sentence on Tan Chun Seng was unduly excessive, and his punishment was substituted with a 10-year prison sentence backdated to the time when he was first arrested.

An Unsolved Murder, *Pennsylvania, USA 2001*

Randall Buchanan, a 42-year-old divorced Deaf handyman from Altoona, a town some 95 miles from Pittsburgh, was known to local people as a likeable person who frequented Shaw's, a tavern three blocks from where he lived alone.

Randall, known as Randy to his friends, liked to play darts in the bar and had an intimate circle of friends not bothered by the fact he was Deaf. There were two petitions for protection from abuse orders laid against him in the five years prior to 2002, one from an ex-wife and the other from an ex-girlfriend which portrayed him as a man given to shoving and hitting, and at odds to how his friends knew him.

Altoona is the home of Penn State University, whose football team was followed and supported avidly by Randy.

On Thursday 21 June 2001, Randy left Shaw's at about 2.15 a.m where he had spent the evening and early hours drinking moderately and talking with other patrons. He could read their lips, and carried a notebook for written communication.

The next afternoon, his new girlfriend went to his cramped apartment after he had failed to turn up at a pre-arranged meeting place and discovered him lying face-down in his living room.

Blair County Coroner Patricia Ross estimated that Randy Buchanan died at around 3 a.m., only 45 minutes after he had left Shaw's. Inexplicitly, the Blair County District Attorney would only say that Randy suffered at least two blunt-force traumas to his "upper extremities", which killed him swiftly and sealed the autopsy report, which after two years was still not released to the public despite a campaign by a local newspaper to have the report released. The grounds on which refusal to release the contents of the report was stated to be that the release of information would jeopardise the investigation.

"*The law does not recognise the possibility of jeopardising a continuing criminal investigation as a proper reason to seal an autopsy report,*" a judge stated when granting a release order to the newspaper. Despite this, the autopsy report has continued to be sealed.

Rumours were rife that a couple on trial for murder of another couple in Maryland, and subsequently sentenced to life (the man) and 20 years (the woman) were regarded as suspects in Randy Buchanan's murder. The man was an ex-Navy Seal, trained in unarmed combat and the couple were suspected of a series of burglaries in Altoona. The scenario was that Randy surprised them in the act of burglarising his apartment on his return from Shaw's, and was killed by the man using techniques learnt from his time as a Navy Seal.

However, the couple in Maryland were never questioned about Buchanan's murder which still remains unsolved.

Randy Buchanan, and his gravestone.

Teenage Cattle herders shot dead, *As Sadah, Iraq,2007*

In times of war, there will be accidents and other incidents where civilians and perhaps also other soldiers of the same side are killed by what is termed as friendly fire. Unfortunately, there are also incidents of deliberate shootings of unarmed villagers, and other civilians. The most famous of this is the Vietnam case of the My Lai Massacre on 16 March 1968 when 347 unarmed men, women and children were killed by soldiers of the Company C of the 1st Battalion, 20th Infantry Regiment, 11th Brigade of the 23rd (Americal) Infantry Division. A platoon leader of this company that gave the order and oversaw the massacre, 2nd Lieutenant William Calley, was subsequently convicted and given a life sentence but was released by President Nixon and served only a 3½ year house arrest sentence.

Some of the civilians killed in the My Lai Massacre
Photo: Wikipedia

Move forward nearly 40 years to March 2007. A different country and a different battleground - Iraq.

On March 6, 2007, an eight-man reconnaissance team led by Staff Sergeant Michael Barbera was deployed into a palm grove about 300 yards from a road known to the US Military as 'Blue Babe'. In the palm grove, they planned to remain secreted for two to three days monitoring possible Iraqi insurgent activity. Shortly before noon, one of the squad, Spc. Finck, reported quietly to the rest of the squad that there were cows approaching their position. Shortly afterwards, the squad spotted two teenage boys moving amongst the cattle and waving their hands and arms to each other. Staff Sergeant Barbera rose onto his knees from his squad's position in high grass among the palm grove and shot the two teenage boys.

One of them pitched forward with a shot in his back and the other quickly raised his arms. This did not prevent him from being hit directly in the centre of the chest by Barbera. After these killings, the squad away from their position and found themselves on a goat path where they spotted a third boy walking towards them looking for the cattle herders.

Pruning shears held in what looked like a military style belt around the boy's waist convinced the soldiers that this was an insurgent and the Army staff sergeant ordered his soldiers to shoot. Three of the soldiers fired their weapons and the third boy dropped dead to the ground.

The noise of the gunfire reached the nearby farming village where these boys had come from, and Barbera ordered the squad to run for it through the palm grove back towards the road, where an army truck was arriving. The rapid withdrawal dangerously exposed some of Barbera's squad to gunfire coming from a village compound as Barbera had not thought to provide cover for his squad's withdrawal. This appalling infringement of standard military practice made some of his soldiers angry as they reported back to their base, but Barbera would report to his superiors that the three dead boys were insurgents operating out of the farming village about 50 miles northeast of Baghdad.

Staff Sergeant Michael Barbera

It was only when a group of angry and bereaved villagers approached the US Military to report the shootings that the full extent of the tragedy became known. All three so-called-insurgents were unarmed. To make things worse, the hand and arm waving that the soldiers had seen were simply gestures of communication as all three boys were Deaf and used Iraqi sign language.

The victims were Ahmad Khalid al-Timmimi, 15, his brother, Abbas al-Timmimi, 14, and their cousin, Muhamed Khaleel Kareem al-Galyani, also 14. They had no known ties to the insurgency.

A photograph taken of two of the soldiers of the reconnaissance team minutes before the two Iraqi brothers were shot in the palm grove. Their faces are obscured to protect their identities.

Their slayings angered most members of Barbera's squad, all decorated combat veterans who subsequently reported the killings to Army investigators in Fort Bragg, North Carolina.

Those soldiers believed Barbera's actions triggered two reprisal suicide bombings at their combat outpost that killed 10 of their fellow paratroopers in the 5th Squadron of the 73rd Cavalry Airborne Reconnaissance Regiment.

In late 2010, several of Barbera's former soldiers asked a newspaper to get answers about what happened to a secret Army probe into their allegations.

In a two-year investigation, a reporter travelled to Fort Bragg, across the United States and into an area of Iraq vacated by American troops to find out what had happened. Classified documents eventually revealed what no soldier or Iraqi villager knew: Army investigators had recommended that Barbera face charges, including two counts of murder.

It was not until November 2013 that Michael Barbera, 31, who was later promoted to sergeant first class, faced the recommended two murder charges and an obstruction of justice charge. Barbera was also charged with lying to his commanders, directing fellow soldiers to lie to military investigators and making a threatening phone call to a civilian in an effort to keep what happened from becoming public.

Sergeant First Class Michael Barbera

However, in October 2014, the Army dropped the murder charges against Michael Barbera in the shooting of two unarmed Iraqi boys during a blown reconnaissance mission in 2007, but he still faced prosecution on allegations that he obstructed the investigation and threatened a journalist's wife.

The murder charges were dropped against Sergeant 1st Class Michael Barbera after I Corps Commander Lt. Gen. Stephen Lanza at the Lewis-McChord Joint Base in Tacoma, Washington had reviewed the results of a pre-trial hearing held last spring.

The results of the hearing have not been made public, but it is believed that the interests of natural justice would not be served if no-one was able to investigate and substantiate evidence from As Sadah in Iraq, as this was now in the hands of the Islamic State.

As of January 2015, Barbera has not been brought to trial to answer the other charges against him. These could potentially lead to an 8-year prison term if Barbera is found guilty.

He changed his name but not his depravity, *Christchurch, New Zealand, 2007*

The popular young woman who worked for the Deaf association of New Zealand wanted to sell her red Mazda Familia car, and like many others, advertised it in local newspapers with a cellphone number, making it clear that she wanted responses in text messages. This was due to the fact she was Deaf.

On the morning of Thursday November 15 2007, Emma signed to her flatmate, Zena Harker, that she might have a prospective buyer, then texted her brother Toby continuously during the morning up to about 11 a.m. describing how she was going to meet the prospective buyer. Like many Deaf people, Emma used her cellphone not only to keep in contact but also to keep her family, who were all also Deaf, informed as to her whereabouts.

Emma's mother, aunt and brother Toby sent several text messages to Emma's phone during the day, as did Zena Harker. All became increasingly concerned about the lack of response to their messages. This was unusual because Emma was usually quite prompt in responding to text messages. Zena Harker even went to the Deaf Club as she knew Emma was on duty that night, but she was not there, and sent a final text message, "What's up, what's up?" but received no reply.

Emma Agnew

After 8 pm, concerned members of Emma's family went to the police station with a sign language interpreter to report her missing. While they were there, they learnt through the interpreter overhearing police conversations that Emma's car had been found at Bromley Park, which was about two kilometres from the centre of Christchurch.

Attempts had been made to set the car on fire, without causing too much damage to the exterior where police forensic experts were later able to extract fingerprints from the rear of the car.

Emma's red car, surrounded by police evidence tape, together with a picture of Emma herself, used by the police to appeal for information.

On November 26, a man walking his dog in the Burwood Plantation near Spencer Park, 5 kilometres north-east of Christchurch city centre, discovered a body hidden in some foliage. This was subsequently identified as the missing girl, Emma Louise Agnew. She was naked, and a sock had been stuffed into her mouth. She was later found to have severe bruises to her neck and her genital area. There was no trace of the clothes she had been wearing.

When her body was found, police already knew who they were looking for through the fingerprints and DNA found on the car. The DNA was further confirmed through extractions of semen found on Emma's body, and the next day, police, acting on a tip off, descended on a motel unit at Wigram Lodge, not far from where Emma's body had been found. Using a battering ram, followed by the insertion of explosive devices which deafened and disabled the occupants, police stormed inside and arrested a man. A woman found in the room was also taken away.

Police identified the man as Liam James Reid. Brought to court for a preliminary hearing, the police van drove through a crowd full of angry people.

Bystanders show their anger as Liam Reid is brought to court.

Liam Reid had been born Julian Heath Edgecombe in 1972 to parents who abandoned him when he was three years old and as Julian Edgecombe, Reid had a long record of assaults, possessing firearms and making threats of murder, as well as robberies and drug offences. In all, he had 61 convictions.

In October 2002, he went on trial for abducting a woman, sexually violating her, and attempting to murder her during a session of experimental sex he described as ""hard out, furious, fast, deviant, experimental, disgusting sex. It was cool. To us it was normal."

He was acquitted of all those charges, but convicted of fraudulently using the victim's bank card while he was on the run, when he knew she had gone to the police. Edgecombe said the sex with her involving spanking and asphyxia using a power cord. He denied that he had tried to hang her with a phone cable. The victim agreed, writing a note, saying she had not been raped and referring to the sex as spanking

After being acquitted on all the sex charges, he was remanded for sentence on the bank card charge and got a three-month jail term. However, his time in prison on remand was marked with serious violence.

In November 2002 he admitted attacking two other prison inmates in a frenzied bashing with a broom handle. He broke the broom handle over one man, who was struck repeatedly. The second victim was bashed over the head when he tried to intervene. This earned him an additional jail sentence of 27 months.

Edgecombe was acquitted in 2003 on a charge of assaulting another inmate with intent to injure - a charge that alleged he had thrown a mug of boiling water in the other man's face and then punched him 15 times. The paedophile - in jail for molesting five children at a church camp - became eligible for tens of thousands of dollars in compensation for the injuries suffered from the beating by Edgecombe. This incident landed him more jail time, and a prison officer lost his job over the incident.

This was the man who had been arrested for the murder of Emma Agnew. When he came up for trial under his new name of Liam Reid, an additional charge was made against him for the robbery and rape of another woman in Dunedin, 310 kilometres south of Christchurch. This woman told of being attacked in the street by a man who put a rope around her neck and choked her during the rape. She had escaped from him by managing to kick him in the testicles causing him to double-up in pain and let her go. DNA found on this woman was matched to Liam Reid.

During the trial in October 2008 at which Reid pleaded not guilty, the court was told that police had managed to track the cellphones of both Reid and Emma Agnew from cellphone tower signals to the suburb of Spencerville, then back to Christchurch. The court also heard that Reid had travelled to the northern South island city of Nelson on 16 November, the day after the murder, and disposed of a number of clothing items. By then, the cellphone had also disappeared.

Heavily tattooed Liam Reid during his trial.

From Nelson, Reid and his girlfriend travelled back to Christchurch and by November 25, he was staying at a place called Wigram Lodge in Christchurch with his girlfriend. The day before on 24 November, he had attacked the other woman in Dunedin, dragging her by her hair across a car park, wrapping a rope around her neck and subjecting her to a prolonged rape ordeal before the victim managed to hit him hard in the testicles and escape.

The Crown alleged that the "rough sex" that Reid employed with Emma Agnew and the woman in Dunedin were a 'signature' of how Reid behaved during sex. This mirrored the evidence presented at the trail of October 2002 when Reid, known then as Edgecombe, was acquitted of raping another woman only because that woman had participated in the extremely rough sex that she had with Reid.

The girlfriend who had been with Reid admitted in court she had been afraid of him, and stayed with him out of fear, due to his violence which was also part of his love-making. She said that he had admitted to her he was responsible for the death of "Emma, the Deaf girl." The girlfriend was accused in court by Defence Counsel David Bunce as a liar. was "totally untruthful and unreliable" in her evidence. Bunce said the woman was "not a girlfriend reluctantly giving evidence" but rather she "lost no opportunity to present Mr Reid in the worst possible way".

Bunce said the woman had been untruthful about the pair's sex life. Text messages from her to Reid showed she was a willing participant in their rough sex, and indeed especially enjoyed it.

The court had packed galleries for most of the trial and visitor numbers were high for the two days of closing addresses by the Crown and defence, and the judge's summing up. Many of those in the public galleries were members of the local Deaf community who were able to follow the trial through the four sign language interpreters employed throughout.

During the trial, the jury had to hear evidence from over 100 witnesses before they were instructed to deliberate their verdict, which took four hours to reach. There was audible reaction from members of the public as the six guilty verdicts were read.

As he announced the sentence, Mr. Justice Chisholm told Reid: "You are an evil and dangerous predator. You are arrogant. You seek to dominate particularly women. You are not without intelligence that is one of the dangers that underlies your activities. Sadly, there is not the slightest flicker of remorse."

As he was jailed indefinitely yesterday for the rape and murder of Emma Agnew, 20, and the subsequent rape and attempted murder of a young Dunedin woman, Reid, 36, bowed to the applauding public gallery, and was spat at in disgust by a member of Agnew's family.

Liam Reid looks pensive as the verdicts are being read out before raising his hands and bowing to acknowledge the public applause.

Liam Reid was sentenced to preventive detention to be released only when the parole board deemed him no longer a threat to society. His minimum non-parole term was set at 26 years, the second-longest stretch awarded to a New Zealand criminal.

In July 2009, the Court of Appeal dismissed Reid's initial appeal against the conviction and a second application for leave to appeal was not made to the Supreme Court until February 21, 2011, more than a year and a half out of time.

Reid had claimed there was a late disclosure by the prosecution of certain DNA evidence and evidence of the tracking of the murdered woman's cell-phone which he claimed the defence was unable to review that evidence before the trial, therefore a miscarriage of justice had occurred.

Reid's lawyer told the Court that evidence was not reviewed because legal aid funding had not been made available, hence the delay in deciding whether there were any grounds to appeal.

In its judgment, the Supreme Court also noted: "Nothing has been put before this court which could provide any basis for the conclusion that either the DNA evidence or the evidence of the tracking of the cell-phone was actually unreliable, so that a substantial miscarriage of justice may have occurred. The suggestion that upon a review either of those pieces of evidence may prove to be suspect in some respect is therefore entirely speculative.

"In these circumstances, and in the absence of any indication that the position concerning funding is likely to change, no grounds have been established for the proposed appeal. The application for leave must therefore be dismissed."

Deaf police officer shot dead, *Alaska, USA, 2010*

Tony Wallace was a rarity. He was one of the handful of Deaf people who were police officers in the United States, counted on the fingers of one hand. There are no other known Deaf police officers anywhere else in the world.

His father and uncle before him had also been police officers, and for as long as anyone could remember, Tony Wallace had wanted to be one himself. A Hall of Fame wrestler while attending Rochester Institute of Technology and the National Technical Institute for the Deaf, he worked as a Public Safety Officer from 2003 to 2006 at RIT until learning of a job with a four-man police department in tiny Hoonah, Alaska, a Tlingit community on Chichagof Island, located in Alaska's panhandle in the southeast region of the state. It is 30 miles west of Juneau, across the Alaskan Inside Passage and has a population of only about 800 people.

An avid boater, hunter and fisherman, Tony Wallace packed up and moved to southeast Alaska, even though he had never visited Alaska previously. His biggest worry was how to get his fast-food fix when the nearest McDonald's was a 40-mile plane ride away from Hoonah in Juneau.

In Hoonah, Wallace worked as a Field Training Officer, an Evidence Officer and a Breath Test Maintenance and Training Officer.

On Saturday August 28 2010, Tony Wallace decided to give his mother, Debbie Greene, a ride in his police cruiser around town to show her where he worked. It was his mother's first ever visit to Alaska, and she had only arrived the preceding Thursday evening after a journey from where she lived in St. Petersburg, Florida. The journey had necessitated a number of plane changes and she was tired and had rested on the Friday, so it was her first opportunity to see the tiny community where her son worked.

Shortly after son and mother had started their tour of Hoonah, Wallace spotted up ahead a private car that he knew belonged to one of his fellow officers, Matthew Tokuoka, a 39-year-old veteran of the Hoonah police department and a former Marine.

Officer Tokuoka, who was off-duty, was in his car with his family when he stopped to talk to his fellow officer, who introduced Tokuoka, his wife and children to Mrs. Greene.

A man, who the two officers had arrested on several occasions in the past, opened fire on Sergeant Wallace from a concealed position nearby, striking Sergeant Wallace in the leg and chest, penetrating his vest.

Officer Tokuoka was able to radio-in a brief situation report and then attempted to drag Sergeant Wallace to cover when he was shot twice in the chest.

Although he was mortally wounded, Sergeant Wallace was able to warn responding officers and rescue personnel of the shooter's location. His mother, a trained nurse, ignored the danger to herself and went to the aid

Sergeant Wallace and Officer Tokuoka posing beside a
Hoonah police cruiser

of both officers to attempt to staunch the wounds. Meanwhile, Tokuoka's wife and children hurriedly exited the family car and took shelter behind it as the gunman escaped into a house

Sergeant Wallace was medevacked to Juneau by a U.S. Coast Guard helicopter and died while undergoing emergency surgery at Bartlett Memorial Hospital in the early morning hours of August 29th; Officer Tokuoka passed away just before midnight on August 28th at the Hoonah Clinic ER before he could be flown to a trauma centre.

The suspect, a former Army marksman, fled to his house and barricaded himself inside; the other two Hoonah officers, an Alaska State Trooper and an off-duty Wrangell police officer visiting relatives in Hoonah, contained the shooter in his house as he continued to fire on officers. Responding Alaska State Troopers and Juneau police SWAT teams were delayed by high seas and wind shears, which made aircraft and small boats unusable. A U.S. Coast Guard cutter brought SWAT personnel from Juneau Police, Alaska State Troopers and U.S. Forest Service officers the following morning. A two day standoff ensued and the suspect surrendered after the use of tear gas.

The arrested man was named as John Marvin, Jr., who had previously been jailed for five years for sexually abusing a nine-year-old girl and had a history of run-ins with Hoonah police department officers. Other convictions included assault, failure to report an accident and disorderly conduct. He had also been found loitering inside an elementary school and escorted off the premises. A court order forbidding him to enter the school was not served after Hoonah police officers decided that he had been sufficiently warned.

His discharge summary from the Hiland Mountain & Meadow Creek Correctional Facility considered Marvin at "high risk" to re-offend and would be a danger to any community in which he resided. The report also emphasised that he have no contact with his previous victim or the victim's family and that he should be allowed no unsupervised contact with female minors under the age of 18.

Slain Hoonah, Alaska police officers Sergeant Tony Wallace (Deaf) and Officer Matthew Tokuoka

John Marvin, Jr.

During his arraignment on Tuesday 31 August, it seemed that Marvin did not understand the charges, repeatedly asking "Who's treating Officer Wallace?" It seemed clear that he did not realise Wallace was dead as bail was set at $1 million.

When Marvin came up for his first trial in 2011, he was ruled incompetent to stand trial and committed to the Alaska Psychiatric Institute in Anchorage for three months in early 2012 for evaluative tests.

The differing testimonies from two psychologists who had examined Marvin were considered later by Superior Court Judge David George, who ruled that Marvin was competent to stand trial. This was scheduled to run for two weeks in October 2012. The jury reached its verdict after deliberating for 11 hours on November 3, finding Marvin guilty of the murders of both Wallace and Tokuoka.

John Nick Marvin, Jr. is led into court by two court security officers during his trial at Juneau Superior Court

Sentencing did not take place until April 2013 following legal arguments whether Wallace was technically on duty at the time of his murder. In Alaska law, there was a difference between killing a police officer while he was on duty, and when he was not (as in the case of Officer Tokuoka).

The real issue was that Wallace's mother was having a ride in his police car, and Wallace had stopped when he saw Officer Tokuoka in his car with his family, which included two small children. The officers and their families were therefore "socialising" in the street when Marvin opened fire.

Judge David George found that Wallace WAS on duty at the time of the killing, and that triggered Alaska's automatic 99-year sentence for the murder of police officers on duty. For good measure, Judge George also imposed a concurrent 99-year sentence for the killing of Officer Tokuoka, both without the possibility of parole.

Tony Wallace's mother, Debbie Greene, cries after Marvin receives two concurrent 99-year sentences.

Deaf centre rampage, *Florida, USA, 2012*

As a student at Boca Ciega High School in Gulfport, Florida just south of St. Petersburg in Pinellas County, he showed a lot of promise, playing football and was class president. He also had the lead role in the school play, *South Pacific*. After graduation, he was accepted for admission at West Point, the US Military Academy in New York but instead, he chose to attend the U.S. Coast Guard Academy and served as a Coastguard for a number of years before deciding he would prefer to have a career as a teacher.

He began his teaching career in 1991 at the Dorothy Thomas Exceptional Center, a K-12 school for at-risk children with special needs. By 2005 he was head of the school. In the summer of 2006, Pinellas School District administrators made him principal at the Van Buren Middle School in Tampa. He had it made - he was well-respected and earning $90,000 a year, and tipped as being one of Tampa's top young educators. He was known with some affection as "Mr.G" by his pupils and developed a pioneering scheme called Kids and Canines in which teenagers trained dogs to help people with disabilities. For this work, he won a civil award.

Unfortunately, Anthony Giancola had an expensive cocaine habit, spending up to $100 a day to satisfy his craving and this led to his downfall. Following a tip-off in February 2007, undercover narcotics officers set up a sting at his school, and while he was in his school office, Giancola purchased cocaine from an undercover narcotics officer. After the drug transaction, the officer arrested Giancola and searched his car where he found marijuana and two glass pipes containing traces of cocaine. The narcotics arrest ended Giancola's career, and led to a year in jail followed by three years of probation.

In 2009, Giancola's fall from grace was completed when his wife divorced him and he was out of work, had no home and living on the fringes of society, a mere shadow of his former self.

A year later, St. Petersburg police officers arrested him as he sat in his car outside his wife's apartment at three in the morning, with a large butcher's knife under his front passenger seat. He was charged with violating his probation, prowling, and loitering.

Anthony Giancola as the well-respected Head of a school

To avoid going back into jail for breach of his parole, Giancola agreed to go into a rehabilitation programme run by the Salvation Army, and after a few months, he was given a position as manager of a residential complex. However, he fell off the wagon again and re-started drinking and using drugs.

Caught being drunk at work, he was instantly dismissed. Moving back into his mother's trailer home, he took a job at a pizza parlour and loathed it, continuing to drink and use drugs with money he had stolen from his mother's bank account.

On Thursday 21 June 2012, Giancola left his mother's trailer and drove to Kenvin's Motel in the nearby town of Lealman. The motel was known as a cheap, filthy place seething with drugs and sexual activity. Stoned with drugs and also dishevelled with alcohol, he targeted the door where a prostitute named Leah Irons roomed. Apparently he had visited her before.

Banging on her door, he shouted drunkenly he wanted a good time. He was waving a wad of cash stolen from his mother. When Leah opened the door, she was cuddling her three year-old daughter who was scared of the very large, rotund 300-lb drunken man shouting at her mother.

"Leave me alone tonight", Leah told him. "Go and see Cat in room 8. She has some crack."

Giancola staggered along to room 8 where another prostitute named Catherine Neal, otherwise known as Cat, opened the door. She told him that she did not have any crack, despite what Leah said, but she could go and get some if he gave her the money. She let him into the room while she went off to buy the drugs, but Giancola fell asleep. When he woke up the next morning, he realised he had been taken for a mug and had been ripped off.

Seething with anger and deranged by the drugs still in his system, Giancola drove like a maniac around the streets of Lealman trying to find the woman who had cheated him. He was completely irrational and his rage demanded some kind outlet.

He screeched to a stop outside a building he mistook for a drugs house, and rushed inside carrying an eight-inch knife. The first person he saw was a young man walking away from him. Shouting at him and getting no response which added fuel to his anger, he ran at the man and stabbed him repeatedly in the back. The surprised man fell down, bleeding badly.

Sweating and panting from the heat and his efforts, Giancola next spotted 59-year-old Mary Allis, coming out of her room turning away from him and going to a back door leading to the yard. Like the young man before her, she was totally unaware of Giancola's presence. Again, Giancola struck at her from behind, plunging the knife deep inside her.

What Giancola did not know was that the building was a home for Deaf people. There were five residents still in the building when Giancola entered, and the first one he stabbed, 27-year-old Justin Vandenburgh, was on his way to the kitchen to make himself some breakfast. The second one, Mary Allis, was still adjusting her hearing aid when she was stabbed.

The back door was locked, so Giancola went back the way he had come, then he was confronted by 25-year-old Danielle Gilbert, who had only minutes before taken her little girl round to play at a neighbour's house. Giancola rushed at her, slashing her wildly with the knife. While he was doing this, Janice Rhoden, aged 43, appeared, also on her way to the kitchen for breakfast. She spotted Danielle on the floor with Giancola bent over her, turned to try and escape but tripped over Danielle's legs. Giancola turned his attention to her, jabbing the knife into her arms, buttocks and head. Before Giancola could stab her any further, the fifth resident still in the building, a young man, came upon him, and with several well-aimed kicks and punches, managed to save the two women from further injury and also force Giancola to drop his knife.

The assailant ran out of the building to his car, jumped in and sped off, leaving behind a bloodbath. The shocked young man hurriedly telephoned the police and emergency services on the home's TTY machine (a special telephone for the deaf).

Justin Vandenburgh was pronounced dead at the scene, whilst Mary Allis was grievously wounded and was dead on arrival at hospital. Both Danielle Gilbert and Janice Rhoden were also transported to hospital with serious wounds, and later recovered. It could have been much worse, but for the intervention of the fifth resident.

Still searching like a madman for his stolen money, he returned to Kenvin's Motel where he confronted the owners in the reception area. His T-shirt was drenched in blood, and he shouted at the owners, Kanu and Indiranden Patel, both aged 57.

"What's happened to my damn money? Give it to me. You know where Cat is. Tell me. All the girls here work for you."

"I've no idea what you are talking about, "Kanu said as Giancola started to hurl furniture and things about their little office. Picking up some breakfast equipment and a hammer, he battered Kanu about the head and smashed Indiranden in the face, breaking her nose and an eye socket as she tried to stop him.

Giving up, Giancola ran out of the motel and finding a car with its keys in the ignition, switched cars and roared away from the motel car park.

Both Kanu and Indiranden Patel survived the motel attack, but Kanu's skull was badly fractured and he spent several weeks in hospital in a coma.

Now driving a Ford Sedan, Giancola next drove into the township of Pinellas

Above & Right:

Scenes after the stabbings at the Deaf Centre Home

Left: Justin Vandenburgh, stabbed in the back without knowing who did it.

Above: The cheap motel where Giancola got ripped off and where he attacked the two owners.

Park, stopping outside a house where about half a dozen people were sitting or standing on the porch talking. Winding down the window, Giancola shouted: "I've got three hundred dollars for a woman who will give me a good time!" Taking one look at his blood-stained face and clothing, they told him to get lost. Furious, Giancola drove off a little way, then U-turned and drove back fast, smashing into the porch and injuring several of them.

As he drove away, Giancola deliberately knocked a 13-year-old boy off his bicycle, then reversed to try and run him down. The boy took shelter behind a telephone pole which stopped the car hitting him.

Giancola drove to a nearby Egg Plotter restaurant where he called his mother. Shortly after the call, she and his sister pulled up, put the blood-covered Giancola into their car and drove him to the mother's trailer. When Giancola climbed into the car he said, "You'll be proud of me, I just killed 10 drug dealers."

When Giancola and the two women arrived at his mother's house, she called the sheriff's office. But before deputies arrived at the trailer, he was gone again. A short time later the police found Giancola hiding in a clump of bushes next to a canal in St. Petersburg, and tasered him.

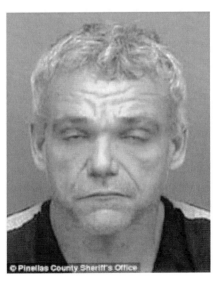

Left:

A dishevelled Anthony Giancola at the time of his arrest, still having the effects of drugs in his system.

In the course of Giancola's crime spree, the former school principal had stabbed four people in the Deaf people's home, killing two of them. He attacked the two motel operators with a hammer, injured four people on the porch, and ran over a boy on a bicycle. The Pinellas County prosecutor charged Tony Giancola with two counts of first degree murder, two counts of attempted murder, and several counts of aggravated assault, and said he would be seeking the death penalty by lethal injection.

But then Giancola's attorneys with the public defender's office offered a guilty plea in exchange for a life sentence. This was agreed to by the prosecutors as long as Giancola received the maximum sentences for each of the eight charges filed against him and that those sentences run back-to-back. The public defender's office accepted this.

That meant that in exchange for Giancola's guilty plea to two first-degree murder charges, four attempted-murder charges and two aggravated battery charges, Giancola received six consecutive life sentences, plus two consecutive 15-year sentences for the two aggravated battery charges.

"You'll never be released from prison," Circuit Judge Thane Covert told Giancola, who was respectful and articulate as Covert accepted his plea and imposed the sentences in Pinellas County Criminal Justice Center on 9 September 2013.

Anthony Giancola receives news of his sentences from Judge Thane Covert

Family members of the victims who were killed — and some of the victims who survived — left the courtroom that Monday with mixed feelings.

"I feel Anthony Giancola should feel privileged that he was able to get life," said Deborah Clem, the aunt of Justin Vandenburgh, as she read from a handwritten statement in court penned by the victim's mother, who was too distraught to read it herself.

One of the survivors at the group home was Janice Rhoden, who was 43 when she was stabbed in the head. "It's just not right he got life in prison," she said outside the courtroom, in sign language that was translated by an interpreter.

"He took advantage of us. We couldn't hear him coming," she said.